MW00791719

Haunted
Southern
California

0 11557 03539 1

Haunted
Southern California

Ghosts and Strange Phenomena of the Golden State

Charles A. Stansfield Jr.

Illustrations by Heather Adel Wiggins

STACKPOLE
BOOKS

To my "Second Family" from Rowan University

Ed and Linda Behm, Bev Currier,
John and Esther Hasse, Dave and Trish Kasserman,
Denyse Lemaire, Jerry and Helen Lint,
Mel and Diane Markowitz, Victor and Maria Rosado,
Laura Ruthig, Dick and Rose Scott, and
Chet and Chesha Zimolzak

Published by
STACKPOLE BOOKS
5067 Ritter Road
Mechanicsburg, PA 17055
www.stackpolebooks.com

Printed in the United States of America

10 9 8 7 6 5 4 3 2 1

FIRST EDITION

Design by Beth Oberholtzer
Cover design by Caroline Stover

Library of Congress Cataloging-in-Publication Data

Stansfield, Charles A.
    Haunted Southern California : ghosts and strange phenomena of the Golden State / Charles A. Stansfield. — 1st ed.
        p.   cm.
    Includes bibliographical references.
    ISBN-13: 978-0-8117-3539-1 (pbk.)
    ISBN-10: 0-8117-3539-7 (pbk.)
    1. Haunted places—California, Southern. 2. Ghosts—California, Southern. I. Title.
BF1472.U6S7275   2009
133.109794'9—dc22

                                                                2008030857

Contents

Contents

Introduction

SUNNY SOUTHERN CALIFORNIA. THOSE THREE WORDS SEEM TO GO SO naturally together. For more than a century and a half, the rest of the country has been fascinated by stories, some true, some fanciful, of California's perfect climate, fertile soils, and healthy, bountiful environment. For example, a popular tale still being told, in some version or other, is that of a newcomer to the Los Angeles suburbs, just arrived from the East. Wishing to build a wooden fence around his new property, he went to the local lumberyard to order materials. "You planning a fence or a hedge?" queried the clerk. "A fence, of course," he replied. "Paint it right away then," said the lumberyard man. Not bothering to question this odd advice, the homeowner built his fence but didn't get around to painting it right away. Sure enough, goes the urban legend, the fence posts grew roots and sprouted leaves, such was the power of California sunshine and fertile soil. Accidentally, he had planted a hedge!

Another tall tale, typical of Southern California boosters, was that of the local family whose brother had died in the Midwest. The body was shipped to Los Angeles so that it could be buried there with the rest of his family. At the graveside, a sentimental old aunt insisted on seeing her beloved nephew one more time. The casket was opened, the healthful California sun beamed down on the corpse, and the body rose up, took a deep breath, and climbed out of the coffin.

Even for those who might not quite believe that California's climate can resurrect the dead, the Golden State is still a very special place. Perhaps this image of an earthly paradise is related to the longtime difficulty of reaching California in the days before jet planes and interstate highways. Early pioneers reached California only after crossing many rugged mountain ranges and searing deserts. California must have seemed like a wondrous oasis after crossing endless miles of desolation.

Is there a dark side of a shadow over this sunny land of healthful vigor and nature's abundance? For students of the supernatural, the answer must be yes.

Southern California has its share—some would say much more than its share—of ghosts and goblins and things that go bump in the night. As with every other part of the country, Southern California's unique collection of phantoms, witches, and haunted places reflects its history and geography. In this book, you'll meet the ghosts of gold prospectors, highwaymen, stagecoach drivers, cowboys, Spanish padres, and Native Americans from California's colorful past. This being Southern California, some of the ghosts are of famous movie industry figures, such as Cecil B. DeMille and Walt Disney. Glamorous spirits putting in an occasional appearance include the specters of Marilyn Monroe and Natalie Wood, with ghostly cameos from Rudolph Valentino, Harpo Marx, and Lon Chaney Sr. UFOs appear in three separate stories. Along with the phantoms of the rich and famous, such as multimillionaire William Randolph Hearst and former first lady Pat Nixon, you'll encounter the spirits of ordinary schoolteachers, police officers, shipwrecked sailors, grandmothers, and small children.

Do you really, truly believe in ghosts? Or are you a confirmed skeptic who nonetheless enjoys stories of haunted places, monsters, and witches? What scares you? Is that strange creaking sound in your house late at night just an old structure responding to the wind, or is it something more sinister? Did you really see a mysterious shadow glide down the hall, or was it your imagination?

If you were to take a little quiz about the supernatural, how would you respond to the question "Do you believe in ghosts?" Would you check "yes," "no," or "not sure?" There are, of course, many who would unhesitatingly check "yes," just as there would be a number of firm "no" choices. But a large number, perhaps the majority, would answer "not sure." Perhaps the unsure would agree with the viewpoint of a wise old man who, when asked whether he believed in ghosts, replied, "No, but I am afraid of them." In other words, he was reluctant to accept the notion that there are ghosts and other manifestations of the supernatural, but on the other hand, he wasn't eager to confront one either.

Are you part of the great group of those not sure, but fascinated just the same by the possibility that the unexplained and the unproven exist out there? Many of those who say there are no such things as ghosts base this on their personal experience—or, rather, lack of experience. They feel that if they haven't seen something, it doesn't exist. This attitude is reinforced by the consensus of most scientists that, since the existence of ghosts hasn't been proven to their satisfaction, they can't be there. Or can they?

Isn't it a little arrogant to dismiss other people's observations as fantasy or deception just because you have not shared their experience? Take, for example, the story of mysterious, manlike creatures living in a remote, rugged wilderness. Described as having some humanoid features, these "men of the forest," as some called them, sometimes walked upright, possessed superhuman strength, were larger and heavier than humans, and were covered with coarse, black hair. These creatures were said to be rather shy of human contact, yet curious about us at the same time.

Do you dismiss these stories as mere tall tales of Bigfoot? No outsiders believed local reports of these creatures, as the observers were not educated scientists, nor could they supply any scientific proof. So these humanlike animals could not exist, right? Wrong. These creatures were "discovered" by the scientific community only about a century ago, in central Africa. We know them as gorillas.

And then there were the tall tales of ordinary sailors, obviously not trained scientists, about fearsome sea monsters. Supposedly forty or fifty feet long, they were described as having multiple writhing arms and great beaks capable of taking chunks out of huge whales, and being aggressive, cagey hunters. These sea monsters were long disbelieved by the scientific community, chalked up as the wild fantasies of drunken sailors. Until, that is, recent evidence convinced everyone that giant squid are very real indeed.

So the "haven't seen it myself, so it can't be" argument doesn't really prove anything. Then there is the fact of universality. Every group of people on every continent has had long traditions of ghosts, witches, vampires, devils, and monsters of all conceivable shapes and types. Every one. Very similar beliefs and descriptions come from people of different races and religions, and are told in all languages. For example, is it only pure coincidence that both Europeans and Native Americans have ancient traditions of "shape-shifting"—that is, the ability of witches or vampires to change instantly from human form into wolves, bats, or owls?

Look at the mighty pyramids of Egypt and remember that they were built to appease the spirits of the dead pharaohs. The ancient Egyptians believed that by preserving and protecting the corpses of the deceased, they could ensure that their spirits successfully journeyed to the spirit world, the land of the dead, instead of hanging around to haunt the living.

Consider also that belief in, and real fear of, witches in the sixteenth and seventeenth centuries led to the deaths of many accused of witchcraft—thirty thousand in England alone. That meant that a lot of people were absolutely convinced that witches were not only real, but also fearsome threats to them.

Do you remain a skeptic? You can still enjoy a good story or two about ghosts, witches, devils, and the like whether or not you are a believer. Many tales of hauntings, witches, and monsters have been part of regional folklore for generations. They connect with the history, culture, and geography of the local area. On the rugged deserts of southeastern California, we encounter legends of ghostly prospectors and miners, while Hollywood has its phantoms of movie stars. With rare exception, ghosts are highly territorial—they haunt a particular place, often a specific room, rather than wander about. And so, in several senses, ghosts are geographic.

For these reasons, southern California has been divided into five general regions: Central Coast, Metropolitan Los Angeles, Mountain and Desert, Metropolitan San Diego, and San Joaquin Valley. The Central Coast region, including the Coast Ranges, runs from Point Sur to Santa Barbara. The Metropolitan Los Angeles region consists of the area from Ventura to Pomona to San Juan Capistrano. The vast Mountain and Desert region ranges from Kings Canyon to Antelope Valley to the Mojave Desert to Death Valley. The Metropolitan San Diego region includes the coast from San Clemente to Imperial Beach, inland to Yuma, north along the Colorado River to Blythe, then west through Palm Springs to San Bernardino and Riverside. The San Joaquin Valley includes the valley and its Fringing Hills from Chowchilla south to Palmdale.

Central Coast

THE CENTRAL COAST REGION RUNS ALONG THE PACIFIC COAST FROM just south of Monterey Bay to Santa Barbara and includes the Coast Ranges. State Highway 1, which clings to the spectacular coast wherever possible, ranks as one of the most scenic drives anywhere in the world.

In this beautiful region, you will meet an interesting variety of phantoms, including shipwreck victims, an eccentric multimillionaire, a famous Hollywood director, and a brilliant musician. You'll encounter a UFO that stalked a woman, a poltergeist that hated cell phones, and the shadow of an airship that crashed many decades ago. Enjoy your tour of the mysterious and dark side of the beautiful coast.

The Ghosts of Point Sur

The coast of California between Monterey and Santa Barbara is one of spectacular, rugged beauty. It is also a dangerous coast for ships, for the mountains of the Santa Lucia Range parallel the coast here, forming many steep cliffs that seem to plunge directly beneath the waves. Only a handful of small towns lie on the sea here, so that in times past, very few lights marked the coast for ships at sea.

Point Sur has a lighthouse, perched at the point's very tip. The light, 270 feet above the churning surf, was built in 1889 and has warned off ships from these cliffs ever since. How the lighthouse came to be built is a long story, and one that involves ghosts.

One of the more tragic shipwrecks at Point Sur, but certainly not the only one, was the fate of the SS *Los Angeles* in 1873. The *Los Angeles* ran aground on a moonless and stormy night, and the storm waves pounded it to pieces. Rescuers the next morning found 150 victims, mostly dead but some still alive, clinging to rocks or floating in the cold water. The local ranchers, who had helped retrieve both the dead and the nearly dead from the sea, had vivid nightmares about the drowned and battered corpses for years afterward. Or *were* they just nightmares? Some locals reported seeing the ghosts of the shipwreck's victims. The ghosts and the nightmare apparitions seemed intent on delivering a message: Point Sur should be marked by a lighthouse to help avoid more wrecks.

The local ranchers couldn't have agreed more. They were tired of being asked to help with the grisly task of fishing corpses out of the ocean and burying them ashore. As San Francisco, ninety miles to the north, grew, shipping and shipwrecks off Point Sur also increased. The wrecks were not without some pleasant surprises. When, in 1879, the ship *Ventura* fell victim to Point Sur's rocks, it turned out to be carrying crates of fine Irish linens, intended for San Francisco's wealthier households. It was said that every ranch in the Big Sur country blossomed with linen tablecloths, dish towels, curtains, and shirts and blouses galore.

But of course, the living agreed with the ghosts of the *Los Angeles*—a lighthouse must be built. Citizens petitioned the state and the federal government for a light. The bureaucratic wheels turned slowly, frustratingly. Well, there would have to be a study made, and committees formed. Recommendations would be made and votes taken. "Don't call us, we'll call you," seemed to be the government's attitude.

The ranchers thereabout reasoned that they could build a lighthouse themselves, but for one problem—the lens to focus light in a single, powerful beam that could be seen far out at sea required a complex glass lens called a Fresnel lens after its French inventor. A lighthouse could be constructed with local resources, but a Fresnel lens would be an expensive import.

In 1889, a new Fresnel lens and associated machinery was delivered to Point Sur. To his great surprise, a rancher living near the point saw a delivery wagon stop at his house. "Is this Pigeon Point, the site of the new lighthouse?" asked the driver. "Why do you want to know?" queried the rancher. "I have your new Fresnel lens, brought by ship all the way around Cape Horn from France!" was the reply. "At the docks, the California Committee for Lighthouses folks directed me south on the coast road." The rancher assured the deliveryman that, yes, this was Pigeon Point, although in reality Pigeon Point was 60 miles north, as the seagull flies. As the wagon driver unloaded a huge crate, he commented, "To tell the truth, the folks on that lighthouse committee were a bit scary. They were very pale, wore sodden clothing, and had seaweed in their hair. One fellow wore a sailor cap with '*Los Angeles*' written on it."

Had the ghosts of the *Los Angeles* wreck somehow intercepted the all-important Fresnel and redirected it to Point Sur? We'll never know for sure, but Point Sur got its lighthouse despite bureaucratic delays. And Pigeon Point eventually got a lighthouse too. Finally, the ghosts of the *Los Angeles* could rest in their graves.

Faithful Even in Death

The role of the Spanish missions in California is well known. Twenty of them were established between 1770 and 1823. They were located a day's journey by horseback apart and were intended to be self-sufficient. Each had a herd of cattle, crop fields, orchards, and vineyards. At each mission, Indians were recruited—some would say kidnapped—as the labor force. The Indians were made to construct buildings, develop irrigation systems, and clear land. They were taught to be weavers, stone masons, carpenters, and blacksmiths.

All was not well with the missions; they seldom reached their goal of self-sufficiency. All too often, the Indians were treated like slaves and abused by their Spanish overseers. Following Mexico's successful revolution and independence from Spain, the Mexican Congress decreed the secularization of the missions in 1833. The Indians were free to leave. Most promptly did so. Times got tough for the missions when their labor force disappeared, which brings us to the ghost story.

Mission Neustra Señora de la Soledad (Our Lady of Solitude) was California's thirteenth mission, founded in 1791. The phrase "unlucky thirteen" could well describe Soledad, named more fittingly than its founders knew. Solitude clearly was its characteristic, as was poverty. It was never particularly prosperous, and the exodus of its Indian workers following secularization left it poor indeed. The mission's last leader, Padre Vincente Sarria, refused to leave, even when the food supply dwindled to virtually nothing. Gradually, the Padre's health and energy declined. Too weak to work in the mission garden, he became emaciated. But he would not retreat. He would not abandon his beloved mission, and he determined not to give up his sacred duty to say mass every day.

The story is that as he approached the altar one Sunday to begin the mass, he died of starvation on the altar steps. Those who claim to have seen his ghost describe Padre Vincente Sarria as lying prostrate, arms outstretched, in the same position he would have taken during the ceremony of his ordination. The Padre remained faithful to his vocation even in death.

The Haunted Inn

The Bella Maggiore Inn in Ventura is a popular bed-and-breakfast where more is served up than just a charming room and gourmet breakfast. At no extra charge, you just might have an encounter with a ghost.

Now a very attractive and certainly reputable establishment, the inn once had a rather shady image. Back in the 1940s, the place was a hangout for gangsters and persons of questionable morals. It was widely rumored at the time that the hotel was also an illegal after-hours bar that served up a full menu of drugs as well.

Some guests have reported catching fleeting glimpses of tough-looking men clad in tuxedos in the downstairs lounge. They have suspicious-looking gun-shaped bulges in their jackets and wear dark glasses. Sometimes they are accompanied by women in 1940s style evening gowns. But when the guests turn for a second look, the images have faded to mere shadows and are then gone.

It seems that frequent appearances are made by a ghost known as Sylvia. Allegedly, Sylvia was a more or less permanent resident of the hotel sixty years ago. She was a prostitute who tried hard to preserve the illusion that she was a casual pickup at the bar, a girl charmed by her clients and motivated by romantic attraction rather than U.S. currency. As Sylvia aged and had fewer "dates," she grew despondent. Finally, one lonely Christmas Eve, when her remaining regulars were home with their families, Sylvia's deep depression caused her to hang herself in her room.

The story is that when Sylvia's phantom appears on the stairs or in the hallways, lights flicker on and off, and bulbs must be replaced every few weeks. Women guests, but not men, who stayed in Sylvia's former room have reported that all the air was sucked out of the room for a moment as they awakened from a horrifying nightmare. Men staying in Sylvia's room, on the other hand, tell of pleasantly erotic dreams. They have no complaints. Everyone agrees that Sylvia's ghost seems to travel in a cloud of the rose-scented perfume that she favored as a living "lady of the evening."

If you stay at the Bella Maggiore Inn, be sure to ask about the story of Sylvia and stay alert for the strong scent of roses.

The Ghost of the Host with the Most

Many ghosts have been sighted at Hearst Castle, but the most prominent one, fittingly, is of the huge structure's builder and former owner, William Randolph Hearst, whose ghost likes to stroll slowly around what he called the assembly room. Eighty-four feet long, thirty-five feet wide, with a carved and decorated ceiling twenty-three feet above the floor, this magnificent room, which perfectly captures the spirit of lavish hospitality evident throughout the castle, was the scene of the host's famous predinner cocktail hours and after-dinner drinks and conversation. In life, William Randolph Hearst was happiest in his role as gracious host and conversationalist, and today the tall, slightly stooped phantom lord of the castle appears to stop repeatedly to converse with mostly unseen spirits.

The fantastic Spanish-style castle was built on a prominent hilltop of the coastal ranges above San Simeon, which is more than 150 miles south of San Francisco and 230 miles north of Los Angeles. The location is significant, as Hearst's business life was centered in San Francisco in the offices of his "flagship" newspaper, the *San Francisco Examiner*, and his social life was based in Los Angeles because of his fascination with film stars.

Hearst's father had built a rambling frame ranch house at San Simeon as a rustic retreat, and the scenic location charmed his son. The vast castle was begun in 1919. The main building has 115 rooms, including 38 bedrooms, 31 bathrooms and 14 sitting rooms. In addition, there are three lavish guest houses, each in Italian Renaissance style, affording special guests luxurious privacy. No one really knows exactly what all this cost, as Hearst kept modifying the plans and adding new rooms. Apparently, he didn't care what it cost, much like a Roman emperor. At his death in 1951, at age eighty-eight, he regarded his castle as still being under construction.

Though Hearst certainly could play the ruthless business mogul at work, after hours revealed a shy and considerate man who drank little and really enjoyed meeting new people. At San Simeon, he delighted in introducing political leaders, such as former president Calvin Coolidge and future prime minister Winston Churchill, to the Hollywood film crowd, some of whose ghosts reportedly make cameo appearances among the phantoms of Hearst Castle.

Hearst's ghost, like the man himself, seems to take a kindly interest in meeting people. It is said that if you happen to be famous in any way, his ghost will approach you, eager to have a nice talk. His ghost also reportedly appears at his Beverly Hills estate, which you may have seen standing in for the home of the arrogant movie producer in the film *The Godfather*. Should you encounter the spirit of William Randolph Hearst, be sure to call him the Chief. That was his favorite title, referring to his role as newspaper publisher. And by the way, don't disagree with your phantom host—he did display a temper on occasion.

The Phantom Musician of Camarillo

The Camarillo State Mental Hospital, which opened in 1936, certainly didn't look a Depression-era version of the institutions known at one time as insane asylums. The buildings are in the Spanish Revival style so popular in California from the early 1900s through the 1940s. Graceful fountains flow in tiled courtyards that look as though they belong in an upscale condo complex. The onetime state mental hospital now is home to a branch of the California State

University system. Today, the hauntingly beautiful, sometimes almost mournful wail of an alto saxophone echoes across the historic campus.

The sounds of the sax, as played by one of jazz's most creative talents, can be heard faintly but frequently across the campus late at night. But this is not the product of some student's expensive sound system turned up a little too high. It is, many believe, a supernatural concert by the ghost of jazz's legendary genius Charlie "Bird" Parker, who once served a six-month sentence in the mental hospital's locked wards.

Charles Christopher Parker was born in Kansas City in 1920. He became nationally famous, even internationally known by the early 1940s. His marvelously creative versions of pop classics, such as "Sweet Georgia Brown," "Embraceable You," and "Body and Soul" established him as one of the greatest jazz musicians of all time. Unfortunately, Charlie became hooked on a fatal rainbow of drugs early in his tragically short career. He started on benzedrine, which he thought would give him the energy needed to play the physically demanding instrument for hours at a time. He soon moved up—or was it down—to heroin. Eventually, "Bird" or "Yardbird," as he was known, was taking a potpourri of drugs.

In June 1946, Charlie wandered into the lobby of Hollywood's Civic Hotel stark naked and playing his sax. Persuaded to return to his room, he lit a cigarette and fell asleep, setting the mattress on fire. His head was so messed up on drugs that a judge sent him to Camarillo State Mental Hospital for six months to detoxify his system, probably saving his life.

Jazz historians agree that "Bird" entered his most brilliantly creative period after his release from Camarillo in January 1947. Was it the clarity of mind induced by a half year's respite from drugs? No one is sure why. However, he soon relapsed into hard drugs. He died in Manhattan in 1955, at the age of thirty-four, his position in jazz history surpassed only by Louis Armstrong.

To this day, his hauntingly creative music can be heard at Camarillo. Try listening late some night.

The Cell Phone Poltergeist

It all depends on how you feel about cell phones. Either this particular poltergeist is an evil demon intent on destroying people's careers and social lives, or it is an avenging angel trying to restore peace and sanity.

A poltergeist, German for "noisy spirit," is the name given to the type of ghost that causes objects to move. Poltergeists typically throw things around, smash china and glass, open and shut doors, and generally make serious nuisances of themselves.

San Luis Obispo, known locally as "Slotown," is a college town, hosting California Polytechnic State University. There is nothing slow about a poltergeist, however, as one university professor discovered at his home in the Mission Plaza area, which features a popular park focused on a wooded creek. Life was good for the family in this very scenic part of the state, with several major wineries in the region and of course, all the cultural events held at the university. Life here was serene—that is, until the poltergeist showed up.

Everyone in the family had a cell phone, even the eight-year-old, who had begged for one on the grounds that she was the only one in her class to be so hideously deprived of the essential tool of social interaction, not to mention emergency communication. The parents caved, so their restored Craftsman-style bungalow now contained five cell phones. At least one seemed to ring every few minutes, and life seemed to be getting more and more hectic. All was not calm with constant communications, which can be annoying.

Then one day, the mother's cell phone went missing. After a frantic search, it was located under the couch. The following day, the father's cell phone was absent without leave. When that number was dialed on another phone, the faint ring tones enabled it to be tracked down in the dusty, little-used attic. But how did it get there? Mom, Dad, the two teenagers, and the eight-year-old all swore complete innocence.

The next day, Dad's cell phone suddenly flew across the room, smashing to bits against the wall. Its expensive replacement was discovered, days later, in the dishwasher—very clean and also very ruined. And then the eight-year-old's much-cherished cell phone was found in the toilet bowl.

The professor's family eventually figured out that turning off the cell phone, at least during family meals and late in the evening, preserved them against the cell phone poltergeist. The professor and his wife, if not the kids, concluded that the poltergeist may have granted them peace and quiet.

Was that your cell phone ringing?

Is There an Underwater UFO Base?

Although dwarfed by today's nuclear-powered carriers, the *Midway* is not exactly small. Launched in 1945, the *Midway* was the first American warship built that was too big to go through the Panama Canal. Tourists can visit the *Midway*, decommissioned in 1992, at the Navy Pier in San Diego, where this longest-serving carrier in U.S. Naval history is a floating museum. The *Midway* attracts many tourists, but none will hear any mention on the guided tour about the ship's alleged encounter with a UFO that appeared to rise right out of the sea. The rumored incident was never officially acknowledged; it may or may not have happened, but it is an impressive story nonetheless.

Several sailors who were aboard the *Midway* that fateful day swear they observed a huge UFO rise out of the sea abruptly, then fly away at incredible speed, narrowly missing a collision with the carrier. They also claim to have been sternly warned against ever talking about the incident. To this day, these sailors insist on complete anonymity when reporting what they witnessed.

Allegedly, the *Midway* was steaming through the Santa Barbara Channel, that part of the Pacific Ocean between the California coast and the Channel Islands where the coast runs almost due east-west. The carrier was off Santa Cruz Island, which is south of the city of Santa Barbara. It was early March 1989, and a late winter storm swept the sea, reducing visibility. None of the *Midway*'s aircraft were aloft; she was in home waters and radar showed no unusual activity.

Just after dawn, the story goes, sailors on early watch were amazed at the sight of a large, unmarked silvery disk rising out of the sea only a few hundred feet away. Sequentially blinking lights appeared to race around the outer rim of the strange craft. It made no sound as it rose to an altitude of about a thousand feet, then raced off to the west. The *Midway*'s captain ordered a flight of

fighter jets to follow it and intercept if possible, but the jets soon lost sight of the UFO. The incident never appeared in the ship's log or any official communication. As far as the records are concerned, it never happened.

Among UFO believers, the waters off the California coast are a notable hot spot for UFO sightings, many of which involve the mysterious craft rising from or sinking into the ocean. It makes some sense that UFOs would use underwater bases to avoid detection, which surely would follow on land. The planet's surface is 70 percent water, so any scientific observation of Earth by aliens should focus on water and undersea research.

Shadowed by a UFO

Many sightings of unidentified flying objects, or UFOs, take the form of brief glimpses of rapidly moving strange lights in the sky. For one woman driving home on a dark winter night, the experience was to last nearly an hour, a terrifying event.

It happened on a particularly lonely stretch of road, State Route 46, between Paso Robles and her home at Cambria on the Pacific coast. This road, shown on travel atlases as a scenic route, crosses the Santa Lucia Mountains and is a truly spectacular drive. For this woman, who wishes to remain anonymous, it was a regular commute to and from her job at a winery near Paso Robles.

The woman, whom we'll call Laura, had worked late and was eager to go home. As she left the U.S. 101 freeway to turn west, she noted a brightly glowing object in the sky just ahead above the lonely road. It appeared to be similar in size and shape to the Goodyear Blimp, but this was no blimp. While it could hover motionlessly in the sky like a blimp, it soon showed that it also could maneuver vertically and horizontally like no known aircraft. The strange object could accelerate incredibly quickly, come to a dead stop, and execute impossibly sharp-angled turns—impossible, that is, for any aircraft Laura had ever seen before.

Over the course of the next twenty miles or so, the UFO appeared to play a cat-and-mouse game with her. If Laura sped up, so did the spacecraft. If she pulled over and stopped, the UFO would hover above her at rapidly changing altitudes, as though preparing to pounce.

Finally, as Laura approached the coast road, the UFO descended to what seemed like only a hundred feet above her. The car's engine died abruptly. The lights and radio went off. An intensely bright light shone down on the car. Laura reported that she was briefly paralyzed. Unable to move, she felt an odd sensation, as though she were being enveloped in a pleasantly warm liquid. This feeling continued for about five minutes. Then both the warmth and the bright light suddenly were shut off. The UFO rose rapidly above her to a height of a few thousand feet and then zoomed out to the west over the ocean, soon disappearing from sight.

As Laura recovered from her momentary daze, she realized that the car's engine was running and the lights were on. She drove home without further incident and since has wondered if it all could have been a dream. Had she really been shadowed by a UFO, stopped, and somehow examined unintrusively? She still is not positively certain about this strange encounter.

The Santa Barbara Horror

Is it possible that a truly horrific crime can literally stain or curse a building? Some folks living in Santa Barbara about eighty years ago thought so.

The legend begins, and ends, with a wealthy investor whom we'll call Howard McGill. He was a successful businessman who had a keen eye for business opportunities and an uncanny ability to judge the future value of real estate. He was one of the first people in Santa Barbara to understand the potential of the motion picture industry. There was a time, in the World War I period, when Santa Barbara rivaled Hollywood as a center for filmmaking. Howard made a fortune in his film studio investments, cashing out at the height of the local industry and wisely investing in real estate. Now, real estate in the 1920s, especially in scenic, fast-growing areas like Southern California, almost took on the trappings of religion. Many fervently believed and prayed that land values would climb steadily upward, ever upward. Howard McGill had a knack for selling at the peak of the market, so his fortune doubled and redoubled.

But as many a wealthy person has concluded, money isn't everything. Howard decided, at the age of fifty, to marry for the first time and raise a family. A year after the wedding, his young wife gave birth to twin boys. Never happier, Howard decided to sell all his properties in order to devote all his time to being a gentleman of leisure and a husband and father. He liquidated his land holdings and alerted his bank that he would be exchanging his very large checks for cash. McGill didn't trust banks, but he trusted his large steel safe at home.

One beautiful sunny day, McGill walked out of the bank with a large leather satchel filled with cash. He didn't notice how awestruck the young teller was who had just handed over stacks of currency totaling more than $100,000. The teller was greedy and ruthless—a dangerous combination indeed for Howard and his family.

The teller looked up McGill's address in the bank records and determined on a midnight burglary. At midnight, the McGill mansion was dark and quiet. The burglar broke in quietly and was ransacking the living room when an unexpected wail broke the silence. The would-be thief didn't know about the McGill twins. Furthermore, a bachelor, he didn't appreciate the feeding schedule of twin infants. As parents of twins know, a nursing mother of new twins can expect to sleep about an hour at a time, if she's lucky, between feedings, diaper changing, and general comforting.

Soon the teller-thief was not alone on the first floor, as Mrs. McGill descended the steps with a loudly hungry twin on each arm. Discovered, the angry burglar struck the defenseless mother a fatal blow on her head with the ax he had used to force open the door. Then, in a horrifically violent rage, he committed what most people agree is the most unforgivable crime there is—the cold-blooded murder of innocent babies. Seizing each twin by the ankles, he swung their heads against the stone fireplace, bashing their brains out.

By this time, Howard McGill had finally awakened from all the commotion. Grabbing his father's Colt revolver, he descended into a scene straight from hell. In an instant, his family had been destroyed in the most grisly fashion imaginable. Outraged, he shot and killed the invader.

Although it would hardly seem possible, the horror only intensified after the triple funeral. A professional cleaning crew brought in to remove all the gore could not rid the house of blood. The blood just could not be scrubbed away. It was reported that blood continued to ooze from the walls, the fireplace stones, and the floor of what came to be known as the murder room. Soap, bleach, fresh paint, new wallpaper—all were to no avail. Howard McGill couldn't bear to live in the house anymore. No one would buy the property after seeing the bloodstains that could not be erased or covered up. Worse yet, neighbors reported that they heard, around every midnight, screams and pathetic moans coming from the empty house. Was the McGill House eternally cursed by the tragedy that had occurred there?

Although Howard planned to have the house demolished, nature beat him to it. The mansion was reduced to a pile of rubble by the Santa Barbara earthquake of 1925. The scene of unspeakable horror was gone forever, though some current residents of the neighborhood swear that around midnight, you can hear faint cries and moans from the site of the former McGill House.

Quiet on the Set

The winds have blown the sand into dunes reaching a height of five hundred feet in some instances. Among the dunes are Egyptian monuments and buildings in the style of the ancient pharaohs. But this place is more than eight thousand miles from Egypt. The sand dunes are real enough, but the Egyptian relics are only about eighty-five years old. They are what's left of a movie set, and they are said to be haunted.

The Guadalupe–Nipomo Dunes, running for about eighteen miles north-south, are the highest beach dunes on the West Coast. The area was chosen by the late, great film director Cecil B. DeMille as the perfect natural setting for his great classic 1923 movie, *The Ten Commandments*. This film established DeMille as one of Hollywood's greatest directors, launching his career as a creative genius. No wonder that his ghost haunts the scene of his monumental epic.

Cecil B. DeMille and spectacular blockbusters based on the Bible were made for each other. His other films include a second version of *The Ten Commandments* (1956), *Samson and Delilah* (1949), *King of Kings* (1927), and *Cleopatra* (1934). His father, a lay minister, sent him to private schools that emphasized religious training, so young Cecil was well acquainted with the Bible. He studied acting in New York and worked as an actor, stage manager, and stage director while writing several moderately successful plays. He partnered with fellow motion picture pioneers Jesse Lasky and Sam Goldwyn to produce films, starting in 1901 at the age of twenty. In forty-three years in the film business, he made more than eighty films, several of which set box-office records and pioneered spectacular special effects.

DeMille's 1923 *Ten Commandments* not only established his reputation, but also remained his favorite film. The first part of the movie, set in ancient times, was filmed in an early version of Technicolor. These were the scenes filmed at the Guadalupe–Nipomo Dunes where the Egyptian film sets were simply left after filming ended. The blowing sands covered them up and they were forgotten until, decades later, the winds uncovered them again.

Today, a tall, imposing phantom figure has been seen striding across the sands in front of the Egyptian-style movie sets. The ghost is dressed in his trademark riding boots, khaki breeches, and broad-brimmed hat. His stern stare is that of a man of action, decisive and demanding. If the phantom gestures toward tourists, they had better move to their assigned places as extras in his biblical epic— DeMille doesn't tolerate onlookers on the set. Quiet!

The Ghost of Morro Bay

A retired science teacher now living in the town of Morro Bay tells her story on the grounds of anonymity. As a scientist, she never believed in ghosts. Until recently, that is.

The lady, whom we'll call Helen, was driving along South Bay Boulevard on a cold, rainy night in winter. It was late, and few vehicles were on the road. She noticed a young woman, drenched and shivering, walking along the side of the road. On impulse, Helen pulled over and offered the girl a ride, which she accepted with some reluctance. The stranger seemed very sad and ill at ease, saying little other than giving her home address. When Helen dropped her off at her house, she kindly lent the young woman a cheap plastic raincoat that she kept in the car for emergencies. Helen hoped that the raincoat, which had her name and address label sewn in it, would find its way back to her, but it was a small loss if it did not.

The raincoat did find its way back to her in a most unusual way. About a week later, an elderly man rang Helen's doorbell. In his arms was the borrowed raincoat. "Is this yours?" inquired the man. "I found it draped across my daughter's tombstone when I visited her grave."

Invited in for a cup of coffee, the man told an interesting and slightly hair-raising story. His teenage daughter had committed suicide exactly one year before Helen's rainy-night encounter with a soaking wet girl. The daughter had experienced, as he called it, a perfect storm of bad news. Her boyfriend had rejected her in favor of her best friend. Her application to enroll in California State Polytechnic University at nearby San Luis Obispo had been turned down. Her pet cat had been hit and killed by a speeding car. Thoroughly disenchanted with life, she jumped to her death off Morro Rock at the northern end of town.

Had the girl's ghost returned to relive her final moments, then begun to struggle back toward her grave when Helen picked her up? "But I took her home," said Helen. "Well, actually, her home is on the other side of town," said the man. "The address she gave was across the street from the cemetery where she is buried."

Helen did not relate this story to anyone else until years afterward. She still shivered at the thought of having given a ride to a ghost.

The Wizard of Lompoc

Folks around Lompoc used to tell the story of the Wizard of Lompoc. Supposedly, Old Man Johnson was a wizard whose extraordinary powers were derived from a pact with the Devil himself.

Fred Johnson had been born around 1850, the child of a Chumash Indian mother and a father who was a failed gold prospector. From his mother, Fred learned Indian lore about magical potions and spells; her brother was a well-known shaman, or witch doctor. From his father, the frustrated and embittered prospector, Fred picked up the attitude that only fools worked hard, that a smart man could prosper using his wits instead of his muscles. Especially if he was willing to bend the rules.

One day, the story goes, the teenage Fred was having a difficult, sweaty, and frustrating day trying to plow a field on his family's farm. The horse was in an uncooperative mood, the harness broke, and the plow kept hitting rocks. "Damn it!" yelled Fred. "There must be an easier way." On that note, a suave, well-dressed stranger suddenly appeared. "What if I were to teach you how to bewitch the plow into plowing the field all by itself?" the stranger inquired.

"What would that be worth to you?" "Anything, anything you want," was Fred's reply. "Sign here, in blood if you don't mind," said the Devil. "This transfers your eternal soul to me on your death."

Fred signed and received in return a beautifully bound volume of magical spells and recipes for exotic potions. Fred became the go-to guy for those seeking supernatural assistance in achieving one's goals—money, love, and success in any endeavor. Did you need magical help of any kind? Fred was your man, for a fee of course. Fred Johnson prospered selling satanic aid to the lazy, the crooked, and the unlovable.

Over the years, Fred half forgot his sale of his soul to the Devil. At long last, in his old age, he took to his bed, the victim of a mysterious fever. As Fred sank into delirium, a knock was heard at his door. Answering, his wife beheld a shiny black coach, drawn by two black horses. The coachman, dressed all in black, announced that he had come to collect Fred's soul, which he did. When Fred's widow worked up the courage to open the book of satanic charms, spells, and nostrums, she discovered that every page was blank.

The Shade of the Macon

The Big Sur country is that part of California coast that lies between Carmel and San Simeon. This magnificently rugged coast runs about ninety miles, north-south, and generally is described as a twenty-mile-wide strip into the Santa Lucia Mountains paralleling the coastline. The spectacular cliffed coast and the redwood forests that sprawl across the mountains make this one of California's top tourist attractions for both scenic drives along State Route 1 and hiking along picturesque trails.

Fans of the supernatural know that the Big Sur coast occasionally features a ghost—a huge ghost, though not a threatening one. On foggy mornings, just as the mist is dissolving in the sun's bright rays, a shadow seems to pass overhead—or does it? It is hard to be certain in this time when wisps of fog still cling to the shadows and low spots. When it can be seen clearly, the shadow appears to be long and narrow, with rounded ends, as though it were the shadow of a huge cylinder. Glancing overhead to discover the cause of the slowly moving shadow, most observers see only an empty sky, while a few catch a quick glimpse of what appears to be a giant cigar-shaped airship, silver in color, moving at a majestic pace along the shoreline. Some people believe that they have seen the ghost, or at least the shade of the ghost, of the U.S. Navy airship *Macon*.

The *Macon* crashed into the sea off Point Sur back in 1935, an early victim of a string of tragedies that ended the era of the giant airships. Back in the 1930s, both the United States and Germany were experimenting with dirigibles (the Germans called them zeppelins). In contrast to the famed Goodyear Blimps, dirigibles had rigid metal skeletons supporting a series of bags filled with lighter-than-air gas. The Germans built passenger-carrying airships like the *Graf Zeppelin*, which cruised completely around the world in 1929. The U.S. Navy used the airships for aerial reconnaissance along the coasts, cruising slowly in search of foreign, potentially hostile submarines. Unlike airplanes, the airships could hover for hours if necessary.

The airships had a flaw that proved fatal to the Navy's dirigible experiments. They were vulnerable to the suddenly shifting winds of thunderstorms. The airship *Akron* went down in the Atlantic Ocean off New Jersey, the *Shenandoah* was lost over Ohio, and the *Macon* splashed into the Pacific. These three disasters ended the U.S. Navy's experiments with airships, but the *Macon* seems to be eternally on patrol. Watch for huge, slow-moving shadows when in Big Sur country. Perhaps you'll see the shade of the *Macon*.

Still in Mourning

Generally, it is unsurprising when fresh flowers appear on graves in a cemetery. What attracted attention in this case was not the flowers themselves, but how and when they were placed.

The caretakers and groundskeepers at the Adalaida Cemetery, located some twenty miles outside Paso Robles, began noticing an unusual pattern of grave decorations. Typically, fresh flowers are placed on the graves of recent burials, on anniversaries of deaths, and on holidays such as Easter, Christmas, and Mother's Day. But here cemetery personnel began seeing flowers placed on a weekly basis, and on a special category of graves—those of very young children. And not just any young children, but those who died about a century ago.

The ethnicity of the deceased, as expressed in family names, seemed to be unimportant to whoever was placing the flowers, so it was doubtful that the floral tributes were from a single relative. Then, too, the approximately one hundred years that separated the actual deaths from the present seemed to rule out family involvement. People tend to visit the graves of relatives they knew very well in life—children, parents, spouses, siblings, or grandparents. Long-dead relatives whom they've never met seldom command much attention.

So who was faithfully visiting and depositing flowers on those century-old graves of unrelated children? What was the common link, if any? What motivated the weekly flower deliveries? None of the local florists' vans were involved.

The mystery only deepened when the unknown mourner was spotted early one morning. It was summer, and the head groundskeeper decided to begin mowing the grass earlier than usual to take advantage of the morning coolness. The lone figure of a woman dressed in white appeared among the tombstones, slowly moving from grave to grave, placing a handful of flowers atop each little child's final resting place. She wore a long, flowing, white dress with a white, broad-brimmed "sun hat" of a style popular in the early twentieth century. Oddly, the flowers held in her arms were all white—roses, carnations, and lilies. When the curious groundskeeper approached her, thinking to engage her in conversation, the woman seemed to startle. Abruptly, she was gone, as though a motion-picture projector had been turned off, leaving only the memory of her image. Was the mysterious visitor a ghost?

The secretary of the local historical society came up with a clue as to the reason for the large number of young children who had died around the time of World War I—a diphtheria epidemic. Today, diphtheria is mostly a grim but distant memory. Infants routinely are inoculated against this once-dreaded disease, but a century ago it was devastating. As it turned out, a little research indicated that the many graves of young children at the Adalaida Cemetery were linked by the scourge.

The mysterious mourner in white remains unknown. Apparently she has adjusted the timing of her weekly visits to avoid any encounters with the living, so she is seldom glimpsed, and then only for a few seconds. The flowers still appear, however—memorials to the dead from a ghost.

Metropolitan Los Angeles

THIS REGION IS RELATIVELY SMALL IN AREA, THOUGH HUGE IN POPULA-
tion. It encompasses the coast from Ventura southward to San Juan
Capistrano. The Los Angeles Basin, the San Fernando Valley, and
the southern flanks of the San Gabriel Mountains form part of the
region's northern boundaries, while a line running from Pomona to
the Santa Ana Mountains to Rancho Santa Margarita forms the eastern edge.

In this compact region, you will meet the ghosts of movie stars,
prehistoric animals, a lost little girl, and a president's lady. The
haunts of ghosts include an abandoned hospital, a pet cemetery,
old hotels and bars, Disneyland, and the classic ocean liner, *Queen
Mary*. Enjoy your tour of the supernatural in the Los Angeles metropolitan area.

The Lady Doesn't Like Progress

The bulldozer's engine roars into full power, then abruptly dies as
the huge earthmover is put into gear. It starts again readily enough,
but then sputters out, repeating the cycle. The same thing happens to
backhoes, dump trucks, cement mixers, and street-paving machines.
Expert mechanics cannot identify the source of the problems. Fuel

lines, fuel pumps, fuel and air filters are all clean and functional. Of course, there does seem to be a tiny problem with the electrical system. Brand new batteries die mysteriously. Wires get so hot that they melt their insulation and short out. Connections get disconnected, as though plucked loose by an unseen hand. Is it sabotage? Well, yes and no say old-timers with previous construction experience in Malibu. No living soul could be blamed. "It's May again," say the experienced workers. "Just keep trying and she'll give up, for a few hours anyway."

This strange "Malibu Curse," which seems to affect construction equipment in this wealthy and exclusive beach resort favored by movie stars and the superrich appears to be the work of the ghost of May K. Rindge. Apparently in death, as in life, May doesn't like development on what once was her private property. While many do not look favorably on change, May positively hated it. The sounds of earthmoving equipment, traffic, and crowds to her were like the screams of Irish banshees—eerie foretellers of death and disaster. To May, construction of any kind—a new road, railroad, or building—was Satan's curse on her peaceful privacy.

It all began when wealthy Fred Rindge, who earlier had made a fortune in manufacturing back in Massachusetts, bought a huge ranch on which to escape the noise and crowding of the mill town where he had made his millions. To guarantee peace, privacy, and security, Fred bought 16,350 acres, which he named Rancho Malibu, Spanish for Deer Ranch. That was in 1892. Fred died in 1905, leaving his dream ranch to his widow, May. May decided to fight any development or construction. She used the courts in a series of lawsuits against the railroads and state and local highway building plans, hired armed guards mounted on horseback to halt construction crews at her property lines, and built high wire fences with barred and chained gates. She even once ordered roads on her land destroyed by dynamite to deny their use to anyone.

You could say that May was not a fan of progress or change. Her own son took her to court, saying that her fanatical determination to maintain her privacy was costing Fred's estate $1 million a year. May's lawyers fought highway and railroad rights-of-way all the way up to the Supreme Court. She lost. Ironically, when May decided to stop fighting the public roads and start enjoying life, she started building a mansion on a hill overlooking the sea, but ran out of money. The unfinished house was a landmark for many years, a monument to May's compulsion to resist change.

Now May's ghost is blamed for any malfunction or bad luck in connection with new construction. May still is messing with noisy machines—and messing with the minds of their operators as well.

The Phantom Gondolier

The graceful, black-varnished gondola, with its traditional high-carved prow, glides down the narrow canal. The gondolier, dressed in the customary black-and-white-striped shirt, black trousers, and jaunty black, beribboned hat, poles the craft along at a slow but steady pace. As is the tradition in old Venice, he sings selections from Italian operas as he propels the gondola through the moonlit evening. It is a very romantic vision, but alas, it is only a vision, not reality. This is Venice, California, not Italy, and the gondola and gondolier are mere phantoms. The image will disappear instantly when a living person comes too close, deliberately or accidentally. This is a ghost, not only of a boat and boatman, but of a dream dating back a century. How a Venetian gondola complete with singing gondolier came to this part of metropolitan Los Angeles is an interesting story, with or without the ghost.

It seems that in the early 1900s, one Abbott Kinney had a fantastic dream of creating a Southern California version of Venice, Italy. Abbott had made his fortune as a Midwestern manufacturing entrepreneur. He arrived in the Los Angeles area semiretired and looking for investment opportunities in the fast-growing metropolitan area blessed with an attractive climate. Real estate prices were soaring, so Kinney determined to create a new suburb, a veritable town that would reflect his cosmopolitan tastes and, of course, make him much richer.

Now, creating an entire community would require a large parcel of undeveloped land—not easily come by and certainly not cheap. But one large tract of land was available and the price seemed reasonable. One problem was that the land was rather soggy. In fact, it was a tidal flat south of Santa Monica. The sellers must have thought that Abbott Kinney was a prize sucker to be interested in this very muddy land, even if it did have an ocean beach and was located almost due west of downtown. An engineer advised Abbott that canals would have to be dug to drain the land enough to build on it. Canals! Kinney had an epiphany—a sudden, startling insight. He had visited Venice on an Italian vacation. Venice's charm and romantic allure were based on its many canals. He would make the canals, necessary to his town-building project on the tidal flats, a major asset in interesting buyers in his new community. In the highly competitive real estate markets of his day, Abbott saw the necessity of having a gimmick—some unique quality to attract potential buyers. Replicating the romantic ambience of the original Venice on the coast of California would be his gimmick.

Kinney saw himself as a man with good taste, and he wanted his re-creation of Venice to reflect his refined tastes. Also, he reasoned, people with high-class interests would likely have matching bank accounts. His Venice would be a high-class town filled with wealthy people who would pay handsome prices for their lots. He built fifteen miles of concrete canals, planning to line them with Italian Renaissance mansions.

Abbott imported Venetian gondolas and experienced gondoliers. They were to ply the new canals to make sure the prospective buyers got the message—this was just like old Venice. The transplanted gondoliers faithfully sculled their crafts along the canals for a while, but few mansions were built. Kinney sold his lots, but to middle-income folks, not millionaires. Tidy little bungalows sprang up, and the gondoliers disappeared. Except, that is, one determined man who continued to navigate the canals on his own time, unwilling to give up his dream job. Is his spirit still out there on the canals, even to this day? Many Venetians think so.

The Haunted Hospital

"Nurse, Nurse!" moans the elderly man in a badly wrinkled hospital gown. "The pain is too great, I can't stand it anymore." His complaints are accompanied by a loud chorus of groans from other unseen but highly vocal patients. Nurses, looking like models of what patient-care professionals wore half a century ago—starched white uniforms, white stockings, white shoes, stiff white caps— glide through the halls. Male orderlies, again dressed all in white, move quickly on mysterious errands.

Except for the rather antique dress code, this could be an everyday scene in any busy hospital, but for one thing—these patients and their caregivers are all ghosts. They are the disembodied spirits of times past, for this hospital, North Hollywood Medical Center, was closed years ago. It stood vacant until the producers of the hit television show *Scrubs* decided to lease it as a set. Cleaned up and refurbished with up-to-date equipment, the old hospital is doing what it does best—looking like a hospital.

Unfortunately for the cast and staff of *Scrubs*, the fresh paint and shiny equipment have not discouraged the phantoms from the past. Many *Scrubs* actors and support staff have had eerie experiences on the set. The show's handsome star, Zach Braff, has been quoted as saying, "I spend every waking hour of my life in an abandoned and haunted hospital." Braff and many of his coworkers are now believers in ghosts, convinced by many supernatural encounters with the tormented spirits that apparently roam the old hospital. There seem to be an unusually large number of problems with electrical equipment, a common phenomenon associated with hauntings. Lights mysteriously flicker on and off. Microphones fail to pick up sound. Cameras malfunction. Many ghost hunters have observed a seeming tie-in between the presence of spirits and electrical problems. Do ghosts create an electrical force field of their own? Does their spiritual energy somehow short-circuit lights or motors? Many have speculated about this electric effect of phantoms.

Why are hospitals, or abandoned hospitals, such well-known hot spots of ghostly presences? Although hospitals are the settings for many positive events, such as the births of healthy infants, successful operations, and welcome cures, they also are scenes of tragedy, death, and negative energies. Those desperately ill or badly injured are taken to hospitals in an often futile attempt to save their lives, so it is not surprising that so many people's lives end in a hospital bed. Their ghosts may remain, perhaps confused as to why they are alone in a strange place. When watching *Scrubs*, do you notice any odd shadows in the background or glimpse an unfamiliar figure? Are moans or groans coming from actors—or from some unseen force? The *Scrubs* crew and cast have become believers. Perhaps you will too.

Ghosts of the Queen Mary

The Royal Mail Steamship *Queen Mary*, one of the most famous ocean liners ever built, sails no more. The great ship is permanently tied up at her dock in Long Beach, now a hotel and tourist attraction in her dignified retirement. The *Queen Mary*, with her long and rich history, sailed to Long Beach on December 9, 1967. She brought with her a supernatural cargo of some 150 reported spirits, for the glamorous liner is also a ship of death, a ship of ghosts.

Launched in 1935 at Greenock, Scotland, the *Queen Mary* was designed and built to be larger, faster, and safer than the ill-fated *Titanic*. Ironically, the hull's watertight compartments, an important safety feature, led to the death of two seamen over the years, one of whom seems to be a very active ghost. The *Titanic* sank because her own watertight compartments did not have caps on them; they were a series of vertical steel walls over which water could, and did, spill into the next compartment if the ship nosed down at a steep angle. In contrast, the *Queen Mary*'s watertight compartments truly are sealed down, triggered by the emergency alarm. Although the *Queen Mary* never was in real danger of sinking, periodic drills for the crew required that the automatic doors be triggered. On two occasions, a crew member scrambling through the doors to reach his emergency station was accidentally crushed by the very mechanism designed to save lives and save the ship. The second victim of these doors, an eighteen-year-old sailor, was killed in 1966. His phantom has been seen racing through the ship, trying to get past the fast-descending automatic doors, which, of course, no longer function.

At least forty-nine people are known to have died on the *Queen Mary*. The most pathetic ghost is that of a baby who died aboard the ship of natural causes. The infant's wails can be heard late at night near the third-class nursery-playroom. During one of the liner's record 1,001 transatlantic crossings, a six-year-old girl accidentally drowned in the second-class swimming pool. Her phantom is said to wander above the ship, leaving wet footprints behind her.

Both the first- and second-class swimming pools are haunted by the ghosts of young women wearing 1930s-style swimwear. They don't appear to be distressed in any way—in fact, some appear to be laughing.

During World War II, the *Queen Mary* served as a troopship. She sailed alone, as joining guarded convoys would have held her speed to that of the slowest ship in the group. The *Queen Mary* was one of the fastest liners ever built, and she relied on her great speed to evade German submarines. She was regarded as a lucky ship, as no torpedoes were ever fired at her. Once a German submarine spotted her off the coast of Africa. The sub's captain had the *Queen* lined up in his sights, only to discover that he was out of torpedoes!

Few knew about the top-secret military execution that took place aboard during the war, an event that produced the only vengeful, truly scary ghost on the *Queen Mary*. A marine on guard duty late one night in 1943 caught a crew member trying to use a flashlight to signal German subs from atop the blacked-out liner speeding across the ocean. An Englishman who was a fervent Nazi, he was immediately executed by an officer's pistol for the crime of treason. It is said that his angry ghost still stalks the promenade deck, carrying his flashlight and menacing anyone foolish enough to approach him.

The *Queen Mary* now offers special ghost tours, though actually seeing ghosts is not guaranteed.

Pet Cemetery

Dog fights occur frequently here, with as many as twenty or thirty canines joining in the general fray. These free-for-alls generally are instigated by the more aggressive breeds—Rottweilers, pit bulls, Alsatians, and mastiffs. Smaller dogs run for cover or lie belly-up in submissive poses, hoping to be ignored or overlooked. Cats sometimes join in, adding to the general confusion. Occasionally parrots or cockatoos flutter about, trying to reach tree limbs on which to perch out of the way. Terrified rabbits and guinea pigs charge aimlessly through the chaotic scene.

How on earth did so many animals, many of them well-known enemies, end up in such a relatively small space? "End up" is the key phrase here, for this is the site of the old Los Angeles pet cemetery, located in the Simi Hills overlooking the San Fernando Valley near Calabasas.

The animals' human companions doubtless envisioned a peaceful eternal sleep for their cherished pets, laid to rest on a picturesque hilltop and memorialized by their caretakers. But this happy vision of loyalty and affection ignored two facts of life—or in this case, death. One is that dogs are highly territorial creatures. They passionately defend their home turf, and in this case each dog's territory has shrunk to a tiny patch of actual turf above its final resting place. The second forgotten truism is that cats, dogs, rabbits, guinea pigs, birds, and a few truly exotic pets such as ferrets and skunks do not tolerate each other in life, and it seems that their spirits retain this mutual suspicion and animosity. Crowd them together in death, and you've got a nightmare scenario.

Fortunately for their living human neighbors, the sounds made by these deceased pets are oddly muted. Only the faintest echoes of all the barks, yowls, and screeches of agitated cats, dogs, or birds can be heard, and that only when the wind is just right. The glowing phosphorescence of the phantom dog fights, cat fights, and interspecies struggles produces blissfully little noise as the ghosts battle one another late at night, especially on moonlit nights.

And late at night is the only time that the animal spirits materialize, as there seems to be a general consensus among the deceased pets not to appear in daylight so as not to frighten or disturb human visitors. The poor pets apparently are so appreciative of visits from their human families that they never appear to cemetery visitors.

It is said that living dogs and cats, with their natural sensitivity to the spirit world, flatly refuse to be taken into the cemetery at all. And the occasional coyote that is either brave enough or stupid enough to venture into the pet cemetery soon runs in terror from the many spirits rising from the grave.

The Isle of Romance's Romantic Ghosts

Catalina likes to advertise itself as the "Island of Romance," and there is a lot of justification for the title, but Catalina could also be known as the "Isle of Smugglers," for that was its main function in the bygone days of Spanish and Mexican rule. Catalina would not use the title "Island of Death," so as not to discourage tourists, but this nickname would be accurate as well.

The island's full name is Santa Catalina, or Saint Catherine. It was "discovered" by the explorer Juan Cabrillo in 1542, but the

Gabrielino Indians had known about it since their ancestors arrived, probably around 500 B.C. The Indians, like many of today's visitors, were attracted by the abundance of fish in the crystal-clear waters offshore. The fish and shellfish also attracted sea otters, whose sleek fur attracted the attention of Russian traders venturing south from Alaska. In 1811, a Russian ship anchored in Avalon Harbor. When the local Indians objected to the ruthless slaughter of every sea otter in sight, the Russians slaughtered the Indians, nearly exterminating them.

The island, twenty-two miles long and varying from half a mile to eight miles in width, is only twenty-one miles across the Santa Catalina Channel from Long Beach. This convenient distance made it a nest of smugglers and pirates. The mists that often surround the island provided useful cover for the fast boats that carried smuggled goods to Long Beach. The smugglers sometimes fought among themselves over their lucrative illegal trade, spilling yet more blood into Catalina's clear waters.

Catalina had a brief gold rush in 1863. Greedy miners extended tunnels out under the seabed in their quest for gold. The collapse and flooding of some tunnels produced more corpses—and more ghosts.

Thus Catalina's first three centuries of post-Columbus history produced three categories of ghosts: Indian victims of mass murder, smugglers and pirates, and drowned gold miners. The shades of the slaughtered Indians are sometimes seen to materialize in the hills behind the town of Avalon as they stand still, shoulder to shoulder, staring out to sea awaiting the return of their Russian oppressors. Boaters in the vicinity of Catalina sometimes catch a fleeting glimpse of a mysterious sloop scudding past them at dawn or dusk, displaying no flag or running lights, perhaps carrying the phantoms of smugglers from the past. And some scuba divers exploring the underwater gardens have reported hearing the eerie screams of the miners trapped by collapsing gold-mine tunnels under the seabed.

The most recent ghosts, as well as the only truly romantic one, are those of the Banning brothers, William Wrigley, and Natalie Wood. The Banning brothers, who once owned much of the island, sometimes appear to guests at the Banning House Lodge, a bed-and-breakfast in the brothers' former home. These nonthreatening ghosts are quietly approving of tourists, as they tried to attract visitors and investors as they worked to develop their property.

The ghost of William Wrigley is said to materialize at his elaborate home at the head of Avalon Canyon. Wrigley, who made a vast fortune manufacturing chewing gum, once bought the whole island, as he was so charmed by its solitude and unique wildlife. Wrigley's spirit is easy to recognize—his ghost is chewing a large wad of gum.

The shade of Natalie Wood, a movie actress famous from the 1940s through the 1970s, is believed to haunt a small cove along Catalina's northeastern shore. Natalie first appeared on screen as a charming little girl in *Miracle on 34th Street,* a Christmas classic, and went on to star in such films as *Rebel without a Cause* and *West Side Story.* One evening, as her yacht was anchored just off Catalina, she either attempted to dive overboard or fell off the deck. She plunged headfirst into a dinghy tied alongside, killing her instantly. Her ghost is seen strolling along a nearby beach. Some say that she died naked. Hers is a truly romantic and beautiful ghost, naked or not.

Suicide Bridge

Pasadena's main claim to fame is the Tournament of Roses Parade, held every January 1 or 2, preceding the Rose Bowl football game. The historic Old Pasadena section brings many tourists, attracted by the quaint shops and restaurants, but Pasadena primarily is an upscale residential community favored by "old money," and one of America's longest established Rolls Royce agencies is located here.

Pasadena also has a darker claim to fame—the infamous "Suicide Bridge." Known officially as the Colorado Street Bridge, this engineering feat stretches 1,467 feet across Arroyo Seco. The awesome drop of 150 feet from the center of the bridge has attracted the attention of a number of people wishing to commit suicide. There is no official count of how many despondent souls have jumped to their death here, but locals believe that the number of resulting ghosts is over twenty.

The first death—and oldest ghost—resulted as the bridge was under construction in 1913. A worker fell fifty feet into a fresh pour of concrete for a support base. As often happened in those days, it was decided to leave the body in the concrete and finish the remaining pours on top. Not giving the unfortunate worker a proper burial almost guaranteed a vengeful ghost, and this angry spirit has repeatedly terrorized anyone who spends a lot of time on the bridge, such as painters and repair personnel. Safety harnesses mysteriously snap, paint cans topple over for no reason, and workers hear a harsh whisper in their ears: "Get off! Get off this bridge!"

A more sympathetic ghost is that of a young mother. Bloodied and disheveled, the young woman seems to be on an eternal quest to find her infant daughter. As the story goes, the despondent woman, having been abandoned by the child's father and unable to find work, decided to throw her baby off the bridge and then jump to her own death, so that she and her child would be reunited in a presumably happier hereafter. She tossed the infant off the bridge, jumping afterward. Miraculously, the baby fell only a few feet into a treetop, which held her until rescued. The mother was killed in the jump, and her tearful spirit now prowls the area searching for her infant.

Other ghosts of suicides sometimes can be heard screaming as they reenact their fatal plunges off the bridge. The bridge was extensively repaired in 1993, and it was finally equipped with a high "suicide railing" to prevent any more deaths—and any more ghosts.

The Mute Ghost

The Beverly Hills Hotel and Bungalows is a very elegant, exclusive, and expensive grand hotel. Located on Sunset Boulevard near Rodeo Drive, it has catered to the rich and famous since 1912. The list of movie stars who have enjoyed its renowned luxury is matched only by accounts of other guests famous in politics, business, and the creative arts. The most private refuges from the public are a series of self-contained bungalows, screened by elaborate plantings and scattered about the hotel grounds.

In keeping with the grand hotel's reputation as a movie star hangout, even its resident ghost is a star—or at least *was* a star. This ghost is mute. It never says anything. While this is not unusual in itself, as ghosts seem to be mute, this is the ghost of a man who in life never uttered a word on stage or on film. This entertainer was an accomplished mime who "spoke" only with an old-fashioned bulb horn and also expressed himself eloquently through his music, for he was a harpist.

The spirit of Harpo Marx is said to appear now and then in the bungalow he favored for many years. His spirit is a gentle one that never threatens or purposely frightens. Most often, Harpo appears playing his harp, which can be faintly heard in the quiet of the evening. Harpo, whose real first name was Arthur, was born in New York City in 1888 and died in 1964. Along with his brothers Groucho, Chico, and Zeppo, Harpo was part of a comedy team that created such classics as *Animal Crackers* (1930), *Monkey Business* (1931), *Duck Soup* (1933), and *A Day at the Races* (1937).

While Harpo's stage persona was that of a blissful simpleton, the rest of the family regarded him as the family intellectual. He was a cultured gentleman, widely read and an art connoisseur, although, like his brothers, he had little formal education. He really loved to play the harp, and did so very well in fact, but never had a music lesson.

So there sits his phantom, gracefully playing the harp, bothering no one. Although many have reported glimpsing his misty image at his favorite bungalow, none complained of being disturbed or frightened. Should you encounter Harpo's spirit, congratulate yourself on having met a Hollywood legend.

Phantoms of the Old Speakeasy

From the dining room come the somewhat muted sounds of patrons enjoying a good dinner—tableware clinking lightly on china dishes, teacups rattling on their saucers, crystal glasses ringing together as toasts are offered. Polite murmurs of conversation are punctuated by louder laughter. All these sounds normally would gladden an innkeeper's heart, except that it is 3 A.M. and the dining room is completely empty—empty of living guests, that is.

This is a frequent event at one of the most haunted hotels in California, the Georgian Hotel in Santa Monica. The Georgian began its career in 1933 as the Lady Windermere Hotel. Now, 1933 was not an especially auspicious year in which to launch a new luxury hotel. It was one of the worst years of the Great Depression. The owners of the Lady Windermere decided that they needed to make their hotel stand out from the crowd. Although Prohibition ended that year, they decided to make the Windermere into a speakeasy, an illegal drinking establishment. It would continue the Prohibition-era appeal of getting away with something naughty, of boldly breaking an unpopular law. The speakeasies of the 1920s had a certain glamour in that ordinarily law-abiding and unadventurous citizens could at least sit in the same room with, if not rub shoulders with, well-known gangsters. The other attractions of running a speakeasy at the new hotel included not buying a liquor license and being able to ignore those pesky legal closing hours.

The owners of the Lady Windermere managed to capitalize on what originally was a drawback—it was somewhat out of the way. Not in central Los Angeles and not in Hollywood, the Lady Windermere made a naturally secluded yet highly accessible little hideaway for those who, for some reason, wanted to avoid ending up on the front page or in the gossip columns.

Many claim to have gotten a quick glimpse of the phantoms of onetime guests Clark Gable and Carole Lombard. Also reportedly present are the ghosts of comedian "Fatty" Arbuckle and debonair gangster Bugsy Siegel, accompanied by his good friend, actor George Raft. The best place to spot these celebrity ghosts is said to be the hotel's Speakeasy Bar.

The Ghost of Marilyn Monroe

The Hollywood Roosevelt Hotel's 450 rooms have hosted many world-famous film personalities, particularly in the 1920s and 1930s when the hotel was an important social center for the movie industry. Located on Hollywood Boulevard across the street from the famed Chinese Theater, with its celebrated collection of footprints of the stars, the Hollywood Roosevelt has seen some ups and downs in its reputation and clientele, but apparently it remains the favorite haunt of some stars long dead. The hotel is thought to play host to some famous ghosts, the most prominent of which are said to be the shades of Montgomery Clift and Marilyn Monroe.

Anyone wishing to meet the ghost of Montgomery Clift is advised to book Room 928. It might help to be a music lover in that room, as Montgomery's ghost is said to play his bugle softly on occasion.

The most famous ghost of the many said to hang out at the Hollywood Roosevelt is that of Marilyn Monroe. This somewhat tragic figure was born as Norma Jean Mortenson (sometimes knows as Norma Jean Baker) on June 1, 1926. Her mother was a film cutter who was very unstable emotionally. Little Norma Jean spent most of her early life shuttling among foster homes and orphanages, abused and unwanted, producing an insecure feeling that never went away, even at the height of her fame. She changed her name to Marilyn Monroe after gaining some success as a photographer's model, including a famous nude shot that was used on the cover of the first issue of *Playboy* magazine. She signed a movie contract, but that first studio didn't use her talents. The contract lapsed, and Marilyn went through a tough time before being "discovered" by another studio. It was rumored, but never proven, that she supported herself as a high-class call girl for a while.

Reserve Cabana 246, once one of Marilyn's favorites, to have the best chance of encountering her ghost. Hers is a tragic, unhappy, though not hostile phantom. Her death by an overdose of legally prescribed drugs at her Brentwood home on August 5, 1962, was officially ruled a suicide. That conclusion was—and remains—controversial. Some believe it was an accidental death, but others allege that she was murdered.

Whatever the circumstances of her death, her ghost at the Hollywood Roosevelt Hotel is a melancholy figure, wandering about the cabana and wringing her hands in despair. The lobby of the hotel contains Marilyn's personal mirror. Many have seen her tear-stained face in that mirror, reflecting her glamorous but basically unhappy personality. One can only pity her and pray that her soul finds the peace she never found in life.

Supernatural Light Show

A family of tourists from New Jersey really enjoyed the free laser light show; at least, they assumed it had been a high-tech light show. They were visiting the famed La Brea Tar Pits in Los Angeles, just off Wilshire Boulevard. First they visited the free observation overlooks, intending to see the neighboring museum later.

As the family members gazed down at the large, open pits of thick, viscous asphalt, they witnessed an amazing visual display of ice age animals in action, something not mentioned in their guidebook. The La Brea Tar Pits are famous throughout the world as the planet's richest source of ice age fossils. An astounding three million fossils have been recovered from the sticky tar.

In past millennia, the natural asphalt—thick, heavy petroleum mixed with rock and both animal and plant debris—proved to be a death trap for all kinds of animals, birds, and reptiles. Shallow pools of water collecting on top of the tar lured animals looking for a refreshing drink. As they advanced to the edge of the water, they became trapped in the ooze and gradually sank into the pits, where the tar preserved their bones. The struggling creatures attracted the attention of large predators, which in turn also got stuck, eventually adding their skeletons to those of their intended prey.

The fossils retrieved here include the bones of the imperial elephant, the largest land mammal that ever lived. Other specimens include giant wolves, camels, llamas, bison, huge sloths, and saber-toothed tigers.

As the New Jersey family watched in awe, the outlines of the ice age animals began to appear in the pit. Glowing faintly with a phosphorescent greenish aura, the unmistakable figure of a saber-toothed tiger was seen stalking a bison. At the moment of the kill, the images faded away. Although no one else shared the viewing platform at the moment, the family spontaneously applauded the very brief but fascinating show.

At the museum's ticket counter, they complimented the cashier on what they assumed was a high-tech light show. "Did they use lasers?" asked one of the kids. "Show? What show? There isn't an outdoor light show," was the reply.

The family members are still wondering exactly what they witnessed. Wouldn't you?

Swallows and Ghosts Return to Capistrano

As is well known, a whole flock of swallows, flying all the way from Argentina, arrives at the picturesque ruins of Mission San Juan Capistrano on the same day each year, March 19, known as St. Joseph's Day. The migratory little birds have nested at the mission since Spanish colonial days. There they build nests, raise the next generation, and leave again, always on schedule, on St. John's Day. October 23. It is said that the swallows were late one spring, but only by four hours, when a storm at sea made flying more difficult.

The punctual swallows aren't the only unusual residents of the mission, however. There also are at least two ghosts.

Mission San Juan Capistrano was officially founded in 1776 by Father Junipero Serra, who named it after a famous crusader. Actual construction on the church did not begin until 1797 and was completed in 1806. In its day, it was considered one of the most beautiful of the California missions, with an arched roof, seven domes, and a tall bell tower that could be seen for miles. Unfortunately for the Franciscan order that staffed the mission, it was built in an earthquake zone. An 1812 earthquake wrecked the church, collapsing the roof and killing twenty-nine people. The church had been in use for only six years. A rebuilding effort in 1865 was washed out when a heavy rain reduced fresh adobe walls to mud. Another earthquake in 1918 destroyed later rebuilding efforts.

The ghost of a Franciscan friar is said to walk through the mission's gardens every evening at dusk, clad in the traditional brown robe and rope girdle. He is thought to have been a victim of the 1812 earthquake. Some believe that if the ghost is seen to be carrying an open Bible, then another earthquake may soon occur. Another ghost is that of a young Indian girl, whose lifeless, strangled corpse was found at the mission on the day the famed swallows returned in 1800. Her murderer and rapist never was brought to justice, despite suspicion that she had been killed by a renegade priest, as the rope around her neck was the same kind used by the Franciscans to cinch their robes.

And then there is the mystery of the bells. Many have heard the mission's great bells ringing late at night. The problem is that the bells haven't really rung since the bell tower was toppled in ruins in the 1812 earthquake. Legend has it that the sound of the bells tolling slowly coincides with a major disaster elsewhere. The mysterious tolling occurred, for example, when the World Trade Center towers were attacked on September 11, 2001, all the way across the continent.

The Ghost of the Chief Who Wasn't

The spirit appears in an Indian-style buckskin outfit decorated in beaded patterns. He is wearing a hip-length war bonnet of eagle feathers and carries a large tomahawk, the very image of an Indian chief as portrayed by Hollywood. In fact, in life, this phantom often was seen on the silver screen as the epitome of Native American bravery and dignity. The reality is, however, that the "Indian chief" seemingly typecast perfectly was not a chief, and in fact not an Indian at all.

The actor known professionally as Chief Buffalo Child Long Lance built an impressive career as a character actor in cowboy films of the 1920s and early 1930s. His portrayals were so convincing that everyone assumed that he was a genuine Native American, a presumption that he encouraged in every way. His film successes enabled him to build a fine house in Arcadia, which has since become part of the Los Angeles County Arboretum. His house and its gardens have become the site of Chief Buffalo Child Long Lance's ghostly appearances. His ghost is said to be a tragic figure, decked out in full Indian regalia, but always with a mournful expression on his handsome face.

The chief committed suicide in 1932, the direct result of a sensational exposé in a newspaper reporting that the chief was not a Native American, but an African American. Chief Buffalo Child Long Lance was a complete fabrication. It is a tribute to his skills as an actor that he convinced everyone for so long that he really was a Native American. In Hollywood, and in all of America in the early days of the movies, few roles were open to black actors. The jobs available were likely to be bit parts as menials or servants, often portrayed in the scripts as dull-witted or lazy. Rather than accept the industry's demeaning limitations on acting opportunities, Long Lance, as he came to be known, decided to take advantage of his handsome face and imposing figure to specialize in Native American roles, for which there was so much demand in the popular Western genre.

The newspaper reporter who exposed his true ethnic identity destroyed the career of the "chief" and subjected him to public ridicule. The devastated actor took his own life and apparently transformed into the tragic ghost still reportedly seen today. How sad that Long Lance was forced by racism to deny his own heritage and live a lie offstage as well as on. This spirit deserves sympathy and respect.

The Phantom of the Sound Stage

The Universal Studios tour is one of the most popular tourist attractions in California. Visitors get an unforgettable insiders' look behind the scenes at all aspects of movie production. Both historic and contemporary movie sets are on view, and demonstrations of special effects are highly entertaining.

What you most likely will not get to see on the popular tram tour, however, is the phantom of Sound Stage 28. This spooky apparition is seldom seen these days, which may be just as well, for this is one truly scary ghost. It is the ghost of one of film history's most effective portrayers of terrifying monsters, Lon Chaney Sr.

Chaney made a series of horror films through the 1920s, some of which became enduring classics. A master mime, Chaney created his own makeup for such outlandish characters as the title role in *The Hunchback of Notre Dame* (1923). His acknowledged masterpiece, however, was *The Phantom of the Opera* (1925). This film created a sensation as soon as it was released. Large downtown theaters advertised that uniformed nurses would be on duty during screening in order to revive patrons who fainted at Chaney's first appearance as the phantom—a public-relations ploy that capitalized on the public's dramatic recoil at Chaney's demonic portrayal.

The impact of *The Phantom of the Opera* is amply demonstrated by the fact that his groundbreaking film has been remade in 1943, 1962, 1989, 1998, and 2004, the most recent being the film version of Andrew Lloyd Webber's stage musical.

The original *Phantom of the Opera* was filmed on Universal's Sound Stage 28, and it is this stage that is haunted by Chaney's ghost. The phantom has been seen lurking on the catwalks high above the stage. Stagehands and actors have spotted the grotesquely made-up face of Chaney in his phantom costume staring back at them before his image dissolves. Often observers see only the back of a black-caped figure running along the catwalks. In life, Lon

Chaney Sr. could frighten the wits out of his audience. As a ghost, he can be even scarier.

If you don't get to visit Sound Stage 28 during the ghost's cameo appearances, at least rent the DVD of the original *Phantom of the Opera*. Enjoy, and try not to faint.

Haunted by James Bond Movies

One would expect that real estate in Beverly Hills would be a good investment. This enclave of movie stars and the superrich is world famous, and homes there are much in demand. So many wealthy people would like to live in Beverly Hills that real estate there would seem to be recession-proof, a fail-proof investment certain to increase in value. Normally, all of this is true, but not for the lovely estate know locally as the Menendez House.

Multimillionaire José Menendez and his wife, Kitty, were murdered in their home by their two sons, who used a shotgun in a notoriously gruesome execution. The grisly event led to a celebrated and highly controversial trial for the two sons. It also led to a haunted house.

After the trial, the Menendez mansion, all nine thousand square feet of it, sold for $3.7 million, a good price reasonably in line with other values in the neighborhood. However, as the new owners learned, their house did not command the escalating value typical of their neighbors' properties. Putting the former Menendez House back on the market attracted few serious buyers. Perhaps the word had gotten out—this house is haunted.

At first the new occupants noticed nothing unusual. The house was beautiful and serene, with no trace of the horrible crime committed there. Soon, however, it became apparent that something was seriously wrong about the den, where the television set would show either a blank screen, no matter what channel was selected, or a James Bond movie. Technicians could find nothing wrong with the set. A new television brought in had the same curious malfunction.

This was a complete puzzle, until it came to light that Jose and Kitty Menendez had been watching a James Bond movie on TV when their lives were brutally cut short by shotgun blasts. Were the ghosts of José and Kitty insisting on reliving their last moments of life by watching James Bond movies? No one knows for sure, but if you buy the Menendez mansion, you'd better be a James Bond fan.

L.A.'s Mysterious Fireball

On June 5, 2004, listeners to Los Angeles radio station KFI heard a very brief report of a most unusual light in the sky. The reporter described it as a fireball and speculated as to whether there might have been a plane in trouble or even a crash. Other than that one brief comment, there was no other news of the mysterious fireball, and no plane crashes had occurred.

No doubt the one isolated fireball report would soon have been forgotten, except that it drew the attention of UFO researchers. Unidentified flying objects are highly controversial phenomena that attract great public interest but also cause people to divide into sharply opposing groups. One contingent is composed of those who flatly deny that UFOs could be anything other than people's imagination. Others prefer to believe that the so-called UFOs actually are misidentified common phenomena—airplanes, orbiting satellites, balloons, meteorites, reflections from clouds, even birds. On the other side are those who suspect that UFOs are real in the sense that no known aircraft could perform the maneuvers or achieve the speeds observed in UFO sightings.

If UFOs exist, are they of earthly origin or visitors from other worlds? Are they the result of supersecret, high-tech research and development by the U.S. government—or, in a really nightmarish scenario, of some foreign government? Or could they really be outer space creatures coming as benign tourists or would-be conquerors?

The controversies about UFOs feed on themselves, because anyone reporting visual or other contact with the unexplainable is likely to be ridiculed as unbalanced, easily fooled, or pathetically eager for attention. Given all this, many who report UFOs soon retract or modify their stories, which brings us back to the June 5, 2004, incident in Los Angeles.

Several UFO enthusiasts contacted KFI radio for more information about the fireball sighting. They were told at first that no such report had been aired. When more people pursued the issue, a station spokesperson said that although the fireball incident had not

been part of a regular newscast, a traffic reporter had spontaneously included his personal observation during a traffic sum-
mary, but it had not been verified. Maybe it was a meteorite, the
spokesperson offered.

So just what was it that had unexpectedly grabbed the traffic
reporter's attention? Others in the Los Angeles area said that they
had seen an extremely bright light in the sky that day, but one that
changed direction abruptly, something that no a meteorite could
ever accomplish. No fragment of meteorite was found, although
this is not unusual, as many meteorites simply burn up because of
friction with Earth's atmosphere. It is likely that many who witnessed the mysterious fireball in the sky on June 5, 2004, decided
to not go public with their observation out of concern about
unwanted and negative publicity.

So keep a sharp eye on the sky. You might see something
unusual. But if you truly see a UFO, will you be brave enough to
talk about it?

Little Lost Girl of Griffith Park

This pathetic little ghost is most unusual in one respect: it wanders
over a relatively large territory. Most phantoms are quite like many
animals—they occupy a specific, often rather small area. Creatures
such as dogs, mice, alligators, birds, even some fish mark out and
defend their home turf. They are said to be territorial—that is, they
try hard to prevent others of their species from infringing on their
home base, the source of their food supply.

Most ghosts likewise are identified with a specific locale. In typical haunted house stories, the ghosts appear most often in one
room or hallway, and these spirits don't wander off down the street
to the convenience store. The case of the little lost girl of Griffith
Park is different, however.

Griffith Park in Los Angeles lies across the eastern end of the
Santa Monica Mountains, north of Hollywood and south of Bur-
bank. It is said to be the largest urban municipal park in the United
States, at 4,218 acres, or more than six and a half square miles. This
enormous park includes the Los Angeles Zoo and Griffith Observa-
tory and Planetarium, but much of the land is still in a natural state.
More than fifty miles of hiking paths wind through the park, and

on many of these, visitors have reported encountering the little lost girl phantom.

"Help me, help me please!" she seems to be pleading, her arms uplifted as she wanders out of the underbrush. Her tear-stained little face is truly pathetic. Some observers have heard her ask for help; others mention a faint crying or whimpering; still other encounters are strictly visual, with no sound at all.

One theory about the lost girl's unusually far-flung appearances is that the ghost was created by the untimely death of an abandoned child, who desperately sought reunion with her parents before dying of exposure. Her spirit thus continues to wander about the vast park, endlessly seeking her treacherous parents.

Some speculate that she is wandering about looking for her abuser, if indeed the child was abused before her abandonment. Little is certain about the background of the ghost. No fear—she will dissolve in mist the moment you see her. Consider praying for her soul.

The Lady in Black

Free. That is a description the gladdens the heart of tourists anywhere, especially in Hollywood. Add together free and ghost sightings, and you have an irresistible combination guaranteed to appeal to visitors.

The Hollywood Forever Cemetery is at 6000 Santa Monica Boulevard, next to Paramount Studios. There the curious can visit the graves of movie stars like Jayne Mansfield, Peter Lorre, and Rudolph Valentino, as well as notorious gangster Bugsy Siegel. But it seems that today's tourists are not the only visitors to these final resting places of the glamorous or infamous. One of the most frequently seen ghosts in the Los Angeles area appears here. She is a very reliable phantom, showing up every day, according to some, and ignoring the living, intent only on her mission of mourning.

The lady is dressed in black from head to toe. A broad-brimmed black hat of a style popular eighty years ago is on her head. A black veil covers her face. In her black-gloved hands, she carries two red roses, which she places carefully at the foot of Rudolph Valentino's tombstone. The ghost pauses before the grave, head bowed in meditation, then disappears abruptly. Anyone bold enough, or unwise enough, to approach the Lady in Black will be met with a terrifying glare from red eyes that seem to pierce the black veil like supernatural lasers.

Once or twice, according to local legend, unwary observers have approached the grave after the lady's phantom had disappeared, intending to take the roses as souvenirs. Supposedly, when they reached for the roses, the flowers leaped at their faces, the sharp thorns tearing at them and leaving bloody wounds.

The ghostly Lady in Black seems like a supernatural stalker, compulsively attracted to Valentino's grave. In death, as in life, Rudolph Valentino apparently still has a magnetic sexual appeal to women.

The future sex symbol was born Rudolph D'Antonguela on May 6, 1895, in Italy. His family brought him to America, where he held such jobs as dishwasher and gardener before becoming a dance instructor. On the dance floor, he was like a graceful panther, mesmerizing women with his trim athletic body and dark, compelling eyes. Rudy headed for Hollywood and used his middle name Valentino as a stage name. His roles as a hot-blooded Arab "bad boy" thrilled millions of woman around the world in movies like *The Sheik* (1921), *Blood and Sand* (1923), and *Son of the Sheik* (1926).

Valentino died suddenly in New York City on August 23, 1926. At the time, it was rumored that he had been poisoned by a jealous lover, who killed him in a rage over his betrayal of her with other women. Is the mysterious Lady in Black in fact the ghost of his murderer? Some think so. Should you glimpse the Lady in Black at Valentino's grave, don't approach her, and don't reach for the roses she leaves behind either.

The Elusive Ghost of a First Lady

This particular ghost is seldom seen, and even when it is, the sighting is typically so brief that the observers aren't sure that they saw anything more than a fleeting shadow. This elusive phantom is said to be the ghost of President Richard Nixon's first lady, Pat.

In life, Pat Nixon was quite shy and self-effacing. She appeared to be somewhat uncomfortable in large crowds, although reportedly she was the picture of relaxed charm in smaller groups.

Like other first ladies who did not seek out publicity, such as Bess Truman, Pat Nixon was underestimated. Despite her shy demeanor, Pat set new records in the number of people she invited to the White House. She supported volunteerism during her time as first lady and even traveled to Vietnam to visit American troops.

Pat was born Thelma Catherine Ryan on March 16, 1912. Her Irish-American father joked that she just missed being his St. Patrick's Day present and nicknamed her Pat. She changed her name legally to Patricia as an adult. She worked as a movie extra to help pay her way through college, graduating with honors from the University of Southern California in 1937. It was while teaching high school in Whittier that Pat met an ambitious young lawyer named Richard Nixon. He proposed on their first date. Pat waited two years before saying yes.

Pat died ten months before her husband, in June 1993, and was buried at the Richard Nixon Presidential Library and Birthplace in Yorba Linda. Her spirit has been briefly glimpsed in the gardens adjoining her burial plot, enjoying the beauty and tranquility of the rosebushes. Interestingly, Richard Nixon's ghost, if there is one, has not yet been observed in Yorba Linda, or anywhere else for that matter.

It is said that frequently people subconsciously choose mates whose character traits balance or contrast with their own. Richard Nixon definitely was a hard-driving type A personality—do it now, not later, and take on yet more work. In Pat, Richard found a smart, hardworking partner but one with a calm, balanced, and controlled persona. Perhaps it is not at all surprising that Pat's spirit takes the time to smell the roses. Maybe we all should.

The Headless Monk

San Juan Capistrano's Los Rios Historic District is a famous haunt for tourists who come to appreciate the carefully preserved old adobe buildings. It also is the haunt of several historic ghosts.

One well-known hot spot for encountering phantoms is the famous El Adobe de Capistrano Restaurant. This fine restaurant is housed in what were once two separate buildings—a residence and the Spanish Colonial era *juzgado*, a combination jail and courthouse. Jails are notorious for harboring ghosts, believed to be because they contain so much negative energy. Generations of vicious, violent criminals and innocent wrongly accused citizens have spent many agonizing hours in such places. Executions commonly occurred in the vicinity, and so it is not surprising if vengeful spirits of the condemned appear in old jails.

One of the more interesting ghosts of El Adobe de Capistrano is that of a monk, who materializes regularly outside the restaurant, dressed in the simple brown robe of his order. He wears leather sandals and a rope clinched around his waist that serves as a belt. Oh, and he is headless. Fresh blood spurts from his thick neck as the body lurches down the street, unable, of course, to see where he is going. Who would have beheaded a monk, and why? The answer may lie in old California's history.

Mission San Juan Capistrano was named after a famous crusader, a saintly warrior. The village that grew up around the mission was as activist and righteous as the mission's namesake. The community actually declared war on Mexico during the early mission days to protest the Mexican government's harsh treatment of the Indians who worked at the mission. No one knows exactly why or how the monk lost his head, but it well could have been during the turmoil of the town's revolt. Was the headless monk a victim of his own government's crackdown on protesters, or was he killed by rebellious Indians for siding with cruel government policies? One thing is sure—the headless phantom can't tell us.

Another famous ghost of San Juan Capistrano is said to haunt the historic Montañez Adobe, built in 1794. This spirit is said to be that of Doña Polonia Montañez, who lived in the house in the late nineteenth century and taught school there. Some say that they've heard the ghostly voices of young children reciting their arithmetic tables while Doña Polonia corrects any mistakes they may make.

The Happy Spirits at Disneyland

"Where dreams come true" is the slogan of the ever-popular Disneyland Resort in Anaheim. Indeed, for half a century, millions of people have gained happy memories here that they remember for the rest of their lives—and perhaps beyond.

Everyone knows that the "happiest place on earth" has ghosts. The Haunted Mansion attraction boasts that it features 999 ghosts, ghouls, and goblins. These phantoms are the products of imaginative engineering of audio-animatronic figures and illusions created by laser lights. What many don't realize, however, is that Disney-land hosts some real ghosts, at least according to some.

The truly supernatural spirits in Disneyland are said to be con-centrated in the vicinity of New Orleans Square. The Disney Gallery, located above the popular Pirates of the Caribbean ride, contains a much-admired collection of Disney memorabilia. Some also say it contains the ghost of Walt Disney himself. In keeping with the spirit of Disneyland, this phantom is charming, friendly, and relaxed. Those who have encountered Walt's spirit described a smiling mid-dle-age gentleman with a neatly trimmed mustache, proudly exam-ining some of the early sketches of the plans for Disneyland. Walt had been inspired by visiting traditional amusement parks with his two young daughters. There he saw that a larger, better-planned theme park would appeal to people of all ages and keep them com-ing back. The dream was born, and apparently Walt Disney's spirit likes to revisit his happy experiences of creating Disneyland.

The Pirates of the Caribbean ride enables visitors to board boats and cruise through a Caribbean port as it is plundered by a jolly band of audio-animatronic buccaneers. This attraction was a major crowd pleaser from the day it opened. It inspired phenomenally successful movies and now displays new Jack Sparrow and Captain Barbossa figures. The ride is said to be haunted, but not to worry—this benign ghost never shows himself to tourists and discreetly rides the boats only during the test cruise done before the ride opens for the day.

This smiling ghost is supposedly that of a ten-year old boy who died of cancer. One of his greatest joys in life had been repeat visits to Disneyland, where he was especially fascinated by the Pirates of the Caribbean. After a ride, he would persuade his parents to get right back in line again. When he succumbed to cancer and was cremated, his parents asked permission to scatter his ashes in the Pirates attraction. Disneyland had to refuse on the grounds of sani-tary regulations, but as the story goes, the boy's parents managed to sprinkle a few grains of his ashes there anyhow.

Every morning before the gates open to eager crowds, a boat is sent through the Pirates of the Caribbean to make sure that it is working properly. This boat enters and exits the attraction empty, but closed-circuit TV monitors show a young boy riding in the front

a wonderful smile on his face. The boy's spirit clearly enjoys
ily private ride, never bothering anyone. For the boy's ghost,
close to paradise.

And Now, Here's Lucy!

Recent inhabitants of the charming house at 100 North Roxbury
Drive, though it may since have changed hands again, have reason
to believe that their beautiful home is haunted. Fortunately for them,
the ghost, if indeed it is a ghost, is nonthreatening and seldom
intrudes on the lives of the living. Although no one has actually
seen this spirit, the family is of the opinion that most likely it is the
phantom of the house's most famous previous owner—Lucille Ball.

The internationally famous and much beloved film and television superstar died in the hospital during surgery on April 26, 1989.
She was seventy-seven years old. Episodes from all three of her
astoundingly successful television series still appear regularly in
syndication, proof of her enduring appeal. Lucille Ball started her
career in movies as a glamour girl, a knockout beauty in such films
as *Ziegfeld Follies* (1946). However, it was as Lucy Ricardo in the hit
series *I Love Lucy* (1951–56), created with her husband, Desi Arnaz,
that she demonstrated her awesome talents as a comedienne.

As befits her television persona as well as her real-life personality, Lucille Ball's presumed ghost has an adventurous, impulsive
side, which is manifested now in restlessly rearranging furniture
and boxes stored up in the attic of her onetime residence. Though
no physical damage has ever been evidenced, householders com-
plain of noisy intervals of movement in the attic. It is believed that
Lucy's spirit is simply following the living person's habit of rum-
maging about in boxes of memorabilia, reliving the many happy
moments of a long, successful career.

One member of the family claims to have heard the opening
theme music from *I Love Lucy*, a peppy little tune, emanating faintly
from the attic on some occasions. No one else has reported this
experience.

Once a former occupant was mildly complaining to an associate
of the occasional rambunctious goings-on in the attic as Lucy's
ghost did its thing.

"Why don't you contact a spiritualist and arrange some sort of exorcism?" asked the friend.

"What, exorcise Lucy's ghost?" was the reply. "Why, I'd never do that. Lucy just wouldn't understand, and her feelings would be hurt!"

This onetime resident still had a strong image of Lucy's character. Lucy, in his mind, was a lovable, wide-eyed innocent with an impish sense of humor and a predilection for overly ambitious, ultimately unworkable schemes. Exorcise Lucy indeed! How could any fan ever think something like that?

So furniture continues to move, and nonmaterial boxes of memories are shifted about the attic. It seems that Lucy is there, reminiscing about her glory days, and who could resent her, much less fear her?

Mountain and Desert Region

THIS SPRAWLING, HIGHLY SCENIC, BUT LIGHTLY POPULATED REGION consists of the Sierra Nevada southward from Kings Canyon National Park to Joshua Tree National Park and I-10 and includes most of California's photogenic deserts. Death Valley and the Mojave Desert are also part of this desert and rugged mountain landscape.

Many of the supernatural phenomena found in this region are as unique and colorful as the land itself. You will meet the spirits of escaped convicts, long-dead Indians, gold prospectors, and gunfighters. The phantom of a steamboat sails on a lake that contains no water. The spirits of vampire cats patrol an almost forgotten camp, and the ghosts of a lost wagon train still roam the desolate desert. Enjoy the natural—and the supernatural—scenery.

The Phantom Convicts of Convict Lake

Convict Lake might seem like an odd moniker for such a beautiful lake, but there is a story—and a ghost or two—associated with the name. Near the Mammoth Lakes district high in the Sierra, Convict Lake is about a mile and a half in elevation and is a popular spot with fishers and campers. Apparently it is also popular with ghosts, as several spirits have been reported here.

On September 17, 1871, twenty-nine convicts escaped from the Nevada State Penitentiary. Most of them were stagecoach and train robbers, but not murderers. Conviction on murder charges in those days was a certain hanging offense. The escapees decided to head west across the California border and up into the High Sierra. This was not necessarily a wise choice, for the first snowfalls in these mountains start in late September and continue into April or May, sometimes June. The winters are hard, with heavy snow. Perhaps the convicts were already all too familiar with the hazards of trying to survive on the harsh Nevada desert without supplies or shelter and decided to try the mountains instead. Why die of agonizing thirst when you could just as easily freeze to death? No one would accuse these convicts of excess brain power.

At any rate, the convicts split up after crossing the state line. Twenty-three of them headed north in the mountains toward Mono Lake, while six went south to the lake now named for them. On the way, they came across a mailman named William Poor. Poor William was murdered in cold blood by the desperadoes when they saw the fearful recognition in his eyes. He had recognized them instantly because, working in the post office, he had studied the wanted posters. This murder meant that the fugitive convicts had crossed the line—if recaptured, they faced the hangman, not just being returned to prison.

Outraged citizens organized a posse and set out for the convicts' hideout, which they reached on September 24. A fierce gun battle broke out, during which Deputy Sheriff Robert Morrison was killed. A nearby mountain peak was named after the sheriff, and the lake was named after the convicts.

Two of the convicts were hanged. One, who had testified against the others, went back to prison, where other prisoners killed him—they don't like rats. Three escaped into the mountains, only to die of exposure and malnutrition.

Two ghostly figures wearing nooses around their necks are regularly sighted near Convict Lake. A third wears a knife in his back; he must be the informer. Three phantoms are covered in ice and snow, with icicles hanging from their eyebrows before their lifeless eyes. The ghosts of Convict Lake can appear at any time, but legend has it that they are most likely to hang out in the fall of the year. Some locals believe that the trout in Convict Lake will not bite at a fisherman's fly when the ghosts are present, so if you are fishing on Convict Lake without any success, keep an eye out for the gruesome ghosts.

The Ghosts of the Owens Lake Massacre

The Indian wars in California that followed a sharp increase in the population of settlers were a major disaster for the state's original people. Between 1849, the beginning of the gold rush, and 1856, an estimated 50,000 Indians died out of an already reduced population of about 120,000 statewide. The main contributor to this near-genocide was a drastic reduction in the Indians' food supply. The newly arrived Americans drove the Indian workforce off the ranch lands and confiscated their traditional lands. The salmon streams on which many Indians depended were fouled and muddied by gold-mining operations.

The Indians retaliated by attacking emigrant wagon trains and stealing cattle. Between 1850 and 1860 alone, the state spent over $3 million fighting Indians. When the Yuma and Mojave tribes persisted in their attacks on white settlers, the invaders drove 100 Indians to a horrible death in Owens Lake in 1865. It seems that this tragedy produced 100 badly disfigured, very vengeful ghosts.

When the 100 Indians were forced into Owens Lake, they didn't drown, which would have been a relatively merciful death compared with their actual fate. Owens Lake isn't a freshwater lake like, say, Lake Superior. California east of the Sierra, like neighboring Nevada, has many dry lakes, products of desert climates where rainfall is sparse. Under desert conditions, most of the rain that drains down the mountain slopes never flows into the ocean. The water simply collects in the lowest depressions and forms huge puddles, which evaporate quickly in the hot dry air. Dry lakes, like Owens, have water in them only after recent thunderstorms or from spring snowmelt on nearby mountains. Most of the time, they either are dry or have only a little water—water that contains alkalines such as borax, which is actually mined from some dry lakes.

Though Owens Lake has no water at all now, its waters in the past were strongly alkaline. They were not only undrinkable, but unswimmable as well. The alkaline water would have produced severe chemical burns on human skin. When the Americans forced the 100 Indians to retreat into Owens Lake, they were sentencing them to an agonizing death.

The ghosts of the Owens Lake massacre are covered with white, caked minerals, with open sores oozing blood. Their faces are contorted in unbearable pain, their mouths open in silent screams. These are very scary ghosts, lusting for revenge. Don't get out of your car at night near Owens Lake. It could be a terrifying experience.

The Angry Cowboys of Owens Valley

Imagine a lush, green valley nestled below the towering peaks of the High Sierra, the tallest of which is Mount Whitney, at 14,494 feet the highest point in California. The streams draining down the steep eastern face of the Sierra provided enough water to keep Owens Valley green, in sharp contrast to Death Valley, only thirty miles farther east. There was a time, before 1908, when Owens Valley was regarded as a cattleman's paradise, but no more. Now it is a desolate landscape whose largest town, Lone Pine, has but 1,655 residents.

Although it is an oxymoron to say that Owens Valley's water was legally stolen, that is exactly what happened. Early American water law, based on English common law, when most Americans lived in the well-watered East, held that whoever got to a stream first had a right to continue using the stream as a source of water. If there wasn't enough water for everyone, then later arrivals were just out of luck. This "first come, first served" rule should have protected the Owens Valley ranchers and farmers against water theft. It didn't.

The fast-growing city of Los Angeles needed to import water to support all the new residents crowding in. Los Angeles decided to tap into the Owens River, 238 miles away. The fact that local farms and ranches already were using that water didn't deter the Angelenos. In a semidesert like the Los Angeles Basin, water equals money, as it permits population growth. Lawyers for Los Angeles argued that the prior use of water by Owens Valley residents couldn't reserve that water for their permanent use when many more people in Los Angeles needed it. The courts agreed, ruling that the greater good overturned the water rights of a few thousand ranchers. In other words, in a dispute over water use, the contender with the most money and votes wins.

Now, cowboys don't give up easily, and the Owens Valley folks felt that changing the law to enable Los Angeles to steal their water, and their livelihood, just was not acceptable. They formed posses to keep their water at home, and to hell with the big city. There was a brief "water war," in which Owens Valley cowboys dynamited the new aqueduct under construction, but eventually the law, and the big city, won. Now Owens Valley looks more like its neighbor, Death Valley.

But the ghosts of the cowboys reportedly still ride out at dusk to patrol the hated Los Angeles aqueduct. Is that just a cloud of dust you see on the horizon in Owens Valley, or are the phantom cowboys out to defend their homes and their way of life? Just salute the cowboy ghosts, should they ride by in the darkening evening. And if you are a lawyer, don't let them find out. Those ghosts really don't like lawyers—or for that matter, anyone from Los Angeles.

A Trap for Evil Spirits

High on a bluff overlooking the Colorado River near Needles is a curious rock maze. Seen from above, it looks as though rocks have been carefully arranged in parallel rows, much like a plowed field. Some of these rows of rocks are at right angles to the others. Further complicating the pattern is a series of spirals and circles, uncannily resembling the mysterious crop circles that began to appear suddenly in both England and America in recent years. It is believed that this rock maze, created by prehistoric peoples, was used for funeral rites. It may have been designed to confuse evil spirits and keep them from following the spirits of the dead on their final journey.

According to local legend, the ancient ancestors of the present-day Mojave Indians believed that the spirits of the dead hovered near the body for a few days, and then traveled down the Colorado River to the sea in order to join with the Great Spirit. The Great Spirit, sensibly, preferred to hover over the sea rather than the land, which becomes almost insufferably hot in this area. Nearby Needles has on occasion recorded temperatures of 110 degrees—at midnight!

The prehistoric Indians believed that all that was good about a person in life was embodied in his or her spirit, while any evil traits and deeds formed into separate spirits that would attempt to follow and harass the good spirit, and keep it from merging into the Great Spirit. Thus the rock maze, painstakingly created over several acres, may have been intended to confuse and trap evil spirits while the good spirit made its escape.

Vandals who might disrupt the sacred geometry of the maze should beware. It is said that if the complex interweaving of straight lines and spirals is disarranged, the evil spirits of the long dead, once freed from the traps contained in the maze, will descend upon the nearest people they see. Perhaps it would be safest to view the maze from a distance. You definitely do not want to risk dislodging any stones.

The Curse of the Rock Carvings

Colossal figures are carved into a flat-topped mesa extending west from the Colorado River near Blythe. These gigantic representations of people and animals were created many centuries ago by Indians using only stone tools to painstakingly cut through the layer of dark stone to the lighter stone underneath. Because this prehistoric artwork was made by incising rock instead of painting with pigments, the huge figures remain as clearly defined today as when they were carved. The only threat to their existence is the work of vandals who might use the same techniques as the long-ago artists, but with modern steel tools.

The contemporary descendants of the prehistoric rock artists, the Mojave and Yuma Indians, are not much worried about vandalism on the mesa. The incised figures are protected, they claim, by a curse that is many centuries old. The message of the rock art, whatever it might be, was of vital importance to the people who created it. It is not coincidence that the massive carvings are close to the Colorado River. In centuries past, just as now, the river makes life possible in this subtropical desert. The ancient peoples called the Colorado *Ahan Yava Kothickwa*, meaning "all the water there is." The rock art, depicting both humans and game animals, may have represented a kind of prayer to the river spirits to send deer, antelope, and buffalo toward the hunters in order to sustain the tribe. Because they were sacred, the figures were under the protection of a curse placed on them by a medicine man or shaman of this tribe— anyone attempting to disturb the figures would die.

In fact, no one did bother them, mostly because no one recognized the aboriginal art as such, until 1932. The huge scale of the figures made them difficult to comprehend from the ground. The largest man, for example, is 167 feet long and 164 feet across his outstretched arms. But when photographed from the air, their true size and shape were revealed. Suddenly the gigantic figures became famous, and unfortunately, they attracted the attention of vandals. That is when the alleged curse came into effect. It is claimed that three teenagers from Los Angeles decided to add some modern graffiti to the collection of human and animal figures. To avoid detection, they approached the figures at night. The next morning, they were found dead, their hearts pierced by stone arrowheads. No one was ever accused of this crime, and vandals have wisely avoided the area ever since.

Are the images really protected by an ancient curse? At least some local people think that the Indian art is enchanted, defended by supernatural forces.

The Phantom Steamboat

The steamboat sails majestically across the lake, black smoke billowing from its funnel, an American flag flying proudly from her stubby mast behind the navigation bridge. Except for her bright red funnel, she is freshly painted a gleaming white. There is nothing exceptional about the modest-sized steamer except for the fact that it cannot be there, for the lake it sails on is Owens Lake, and Owens Lake hasn't had water in it since 1926.

Though Owens Lake was a highly alkaline lake, its waters so loaded with caustic minerals that it was undrinkable and unswimmable, it was still navigable. Until, that is, the city of Los Angeles built an aqueduct to intercept the fresh waters of the Owens River and deliver them to Los Angeles instead of Owens Lake.

Before Los Angeles appropriated its source of water, Owens Lake did have steamboats plying its twelve-mile length. The phantom boat is thought to be the ghost of the *Bessie Brady*, which was launched on the lake in 1872. *Bessie*'s job was to haul silver bullion, gold bars, and timber down the lake to waiting wagon trains. Even after the railroads came to the eighty-five-mile-long Owens Valley, *Bessie* still sailed, as water transportation was cheaper per mile than railroads. The *Bessie Brady* burned in an 1892 fire, so both the phantom steamboat and the lake waters she cruises are long gone—a kind of double phenomenon.

Although the phantom steamboat is an interesting spectacle in itself, many people have attempted to locate the remains of the actual *Bessie Brady*, so far with some success. A three-hundred-pound bronze propeller, which may have been *Bessie*'s, has been dug out of the dry sands that now occupy the former lakebed. A four-hundred-pound iron anchor was retrieved nearby. Some fortune hunters have tried to follow the ghostly steamboat on her moonlit journeys, hoping the phantom would lead them to *Bessie*'s fire-blackened hull. So far, the hunters have been frustrated in their search, but they haven't given up, for it is rumored that *Bessie*'s cargo on her last voyage included a fortune in gold and silver.

So if you should spot a steamboat sailing impossibly across a nonexistent lake, watch her carefully. *Bessie* could lead you to great wealth. Maybe.

Ghosts in the Ghost Town

Calico is one of California's most famous ghost towns, thanks to its geography and its history. Located just off I-15, about ten miles east of Barstow, Calico is very accessible to tourists, whose dollars have given it new life. Calico's history is typical of almost all western ghost towns. It once prospered in the midst of a barren desert because of rich mines. Silver was discovered at Calico in 1881. Over the next fifteen years, the mines at Calico produced $86 million worth of silver, and that was at a time when men worked for a few dollars a day. But in 1896, the price of silver dropped below the cost of mining it, and Calico became a ghost town—complete with sightings of ghosts.

A grizzled old miner leads a burro across the rough ground at the foot of the mountains near Calico, which was named for the brightly colored rocks nearby. The burro is laden with large sacks of provisions, for the prospector is heading back to the secret location of his strike. Many locals have tried to follow the man and his burro, hoping to be led to the hidden mine. They don't succeed, because both man and beast seem to disappear in the twilight. It is no use trying to track their trail, as they leave no footprints. They can't, for they are only phantoms. The old prospector is one of the most commonly seen ghosts of the ghost town.

Another famous—or infamous—ghost at Calico is that of a very heavy cowboy carrying his head under his arm and holding a six-gun in each hand. This grotesque phantom is said to be that of "Fatty" Johnson. Fatty is alleged to have weighed over more than three hundred pounds. He consumed huge quantities of food and drink, and he cheated at cards. His drunken arrogance and obvious cheating landed him in many gunfights, which he usually won. After killing a bartender in cold blood, accusing the man of watering the whiskey, Fatty was sentenced to hang. The whole town turned out for that festive occasion, so there were plenty of witnesses to an unforgettable hanging. When the trapdoor opened, Fatty's huge weight caused the noose to wrench his head from his body. Fatty's head was kept on display at the saloon that was the scene of the bartender's demise, while the rest of his corpse was buried. Supposedly, Fatty's headless ghost rose from the grave, stomped into the saloon, and retrieved his head. Watch out for Fatty—he's armed and dangerous.

Not far from Calico ghost town is an archaeological site where stone tools and other artifacts dating back twenty-five thousand years have been found. Some claim that the ghosts of very early Americans haunt this site. Apparently they are not pleased that their ancient graves have been disturbed.

Seldom Seen Slim

Although Ballarat appears to have a ghost, it hardly qualifies as a ghost town in the traditional sense. At one time, the desolate desert community was a thriving mining town, but even at its height, it never was very large or important. Ballarat was named after the town in Australia where gold was first discovered, setting off a gold rush in the Land Down Under. Gold was discovered at California's Ballarat in 1851, very early in the state's own gold rush. Very likely, Australian miners attracted by news of gold in California gave Ballarat its name.

The typical ghost town features a collection of abandoned buildings in some degree of disrepair, but still recognizable as buildings. Ballarat has no intact structures, only a few weathered boards scattered among ruined foundations of brick or fieldstone. It does have a cemetery, and a few tombstones have survived intact to this day. Not too surprisingly, the cemetery is thought to be haunted, like many around the world.

A visit to Ballarat's cemetery may enable you to meet a ghost. Or it may not, as the phantom is as independent, solitary, and disinclined to welcome strangers as was the living man. Still, if you are lucky, and very quiet, you might just see the ghost of Seldom Seen Slim, one of the most unique and memorable characters ever to call Ballarat home.

Ballarat died as a mining community when the Radcliff Mine closed in 1902, after steadily producing gold for half a century. When the Radcliff closed and the paychecks stopped, most of Ballarat's people left, but not Seldom Seen Slim. Slim was an independent prospector, not on the payroll of the Radcliff or any other big mine. Slim decided to stay behind in Ballarat and keep looking for gold. He was not just a cockeyed optimist. Actually, it is pretty common for anyone looking for gold, or for that matter, any metal ore or oil, to follow the "vicinity" rule—the best hope of finding more gold, or copper, or silver, or oil is to look near where it already has been found.

So Slim hung around and kept looking for gold in the general vicinity of Ballarat. He earned the "Seldom Seen" part of his nickname because he didn't want to be seen. He didn't want anyone following him on his search for gold, and then killing him or at least stealing from him if in fact he found some. Thus even during his lifetime, Seldom Seen Slim behaved like a ghost, quickly disappearing from view when he saw someone nearing him.

Slim cultivated an image of a highly independent old curmudgeon, often remarking to others who asked why he much preferred to be alone, "Me lonely? Hell no, I'm half coyote and half wild burro!" Did Slim ever find gold? The answer is yes, but the location of his strike has not yet been discovered. But find some he did, for the men who came across his body in his rough cabin at Ballarat also found a little bag of nuggets, along with Slim's last will. His will asked that the gold be used to give him a proper burial with a fine tombstone. The gold left after that final expense was to be used to buy rounds of drinks at his wake. His tombstone reads "Seldom Seen Slim—Half coyote and half wild burro and never lonely—until now."

The ghost of Slim—which, true to form, is seldom seen—is said to appear on occasion, seated atop his tombstone and smoking a pipe. Several adventurers and ghost hunters have attempted to follow the ghost when it strolls away, hoping it will lead them to the source of Slim's gold. No one has yet located Slim's strike, but maybe you'll get lucky. Just remember to be very quiet and stay out of sight.

A Town That Died Twice

Ludlow is a place name on the map, but not much more than that. Located about fifty-five miles east of Barstow, Ludlow is in a particularly empty part of the Mojave Desert. Near the present minimal services typical of a remote highway interchange lie the sad remains of what was once a little town but now is a ghost town—a ghost town that, in fact, died twice. Among the sparse remnants of the town that once was is a handful of wooden crosses in the cemetery. It is these wooden crosses that are the site of the haunting.

Ludlow is dry—bone dry. There is no surface water to be tapped for a reliable supply, and yet Ludlow's first reason for being was to serve as a watering stop on the railroad. All the water so vital to the operation of steam locomotives had to be hauled in railroad tank cars from Newberry Springs, thirty miles to the west. When locomotives became larger and could carry more of their own water supply, Ludlow ceased to have any function, and the tiny town died. It had existed only from 1882 to about 1910.

Then in the 1920s, Ludlow found itself reborn as a highway stop when the famous Route 66, running from Chicago to Los Angeles, was built. The need for highway services led to the rebirth of Ludlow. Its reincarnation lasted until the 1960s, when I-50 was built. This new highway ran a ways north of the old route, so Ludlow died again—or actually, the town had to relocate at the interstate's interchange.

Now, a town that died twice is bound to host some ghosts. The site of the old town of Ludlow is marked only by a few building foundations and those forlorn crosses in the little cemetery.

Anyone taking the time to drive from the interchange to the former site of Ludlow will spot these crosses. They were made simply by nailing and wiring a wooden crosspiece to a wooden post. The names and dates of the deceased were painted on the crosses and that was that, a common practice for a quick and cheap burial.

The problem, from the point of view of the spirits of the dead, is that the desert winds and blowing sands long ago erased the paint. There is no way to identify the people buried in that intensely lonely place.

Listen carefully at the Ludlow cemetery, and you may hear what so many others claim to have heard—desperate whispers of names, as the spirits of the dead are trying to tell the living their identity, now that weather and time have stolen their names. It is the ultimate sadness that the dead are anonymous and cannot be mourned. No one can offer a prayer for their eternal souls when all traces of their names are gone. This is an especially sad and forlorn cemetery. It is no surprise that it is haunted.

The Spirit of the Sierra

This spirit has been seen in a wide variety of locations scattered through the Sierra of California, which is fitting, as the once-living person was a renowned wanderer. This interesting, nonthreatening ghost is that of famed naturalist, conservationist, and political activist John Muir. Should you encounter Muir's spirit, you might give him a wave and a smile of appreciation for his farsighted life work of preserving so much spectacular scenery for future generations.

The best chance of catching a glimpse of the phantom of this American legend is in Yosemite National Park, near such notable scenic superstars as Glacier Point, the Grand Canyon of the Tuolumne, or the Mariposa Grove of giant sequoia trees. John Muir's spirit, however, has been known to appear as far afield as the Lake Tahoe area to the north or Kings Canyon National Park to the south.

The ghost of John Muir appears as a rather faded, slightly fuzzy image, often with a faintly greenish glow. The phantom is that of a tall, robust man in late maturity. He is heavily bearded with long, slightly tangled hair, a broad-brimmed hat, and worn but clean denim trousers and jacket. He is wearing a backpack and carries a stout walking stick. Although most encounters with this spirit of the Sierra consist only of a brief glimpse before the image fades into the woods, John Muir's ghost will, on occasion, choose to interact with the living. The phantom may take the time, for example, to kick dirt over the glowing embers of a campfire not being watched carefully in fire season. Muir's ghost also has been said to help lost hikers by pointing in the direction they should take.

John Muir was even more interesting than his reputed ghost. He was born in Scotland in 1838. His parents brought him to Wisconsin when he was eleven. John always was intensely interested in nature and really loved to hike. Once he walked from Indianapolis to Cedar Key, Florida. He first saw Yosemite Valley at the age of thirty, when he walked there from San Francisco. It was love at first sight. He explored Yosemite as no one had before and ended up living as a sheepherder, but he was horrified at the damage to natural vegetation caused by sheep and became an ardent conservationist.

Muir founded the pioneering conservationist group the Sierra Club in 1892. He persuaded President Grover Cleveland to create thirteen national forests and took President Theodore Roosevelt camping in Yosemite to encourage him to expand national parks and forests in the High Sierra. Muir's life work focused on preserving the pristine splendor of the Sierra as parks for all to enjoy, so it would not be surprising if his spirit still strides along the hiking trails, enjoying the beauty that he worked so hard to conserve.

The Gunfighter's Ghost

The tall, slender man is dressed entirely in black, from his boots to his ten-gallon cowboy hat. He walks with a swagger, the very picture of supreme self-confidence and bravado. His dark eyes are alert within a grim visage. He stops in his tracks, his hands held out at his side, twitching slightly as he prepares to draw on his opponent. Then, lightning quick, he draws both six-guns from their holsters and fires them simultaneously. Don't bother to duck—the bullets can do no harm, as they come from immaterial guns fired by a phantom gunfighter. There is no reality here, only a fleeting image. You have just encountered the ghost of the legendary Wyatt Earp, so you must be near his final resting place in Colton's Agua Mansa Cemetery. Not that Wyatt Earp's ghost does much resting. His spirit seems to be as restless as the once-living man.

If one man's life could summarize the romantic image and frequently unglamorous reality of the rugged, adventurous westerner, it would be the saga of Wyatt Earp. He was, at various times in his long life, an outlaw, lawman, gambler, buffalo hunter, cowboy, gold prospector, and saloon owner. You could say he was kind of restless and adventurous.

Wyatt Earp was born in Missouri in 1848. Maybe his short-tempered pugnacity could be traced back to a childhood featuring daily schoolyard brawls defending an unusual name that sounded so like a hiccup to schoolmates.

At the age of twenty-two, Wyatt decided to run against his cousin for town constable in Lamar, Missouri. He won but didn't hold the job for long, resigning under cloudy circumstances. Much of his career featured unclear reasons for leaving jobs and leaving town. Wyatt seemed to swing back and forth between lawman and outlaw. He once was arrested for stealing horses in Oklahoma. In 1874, he served as an officer in Wichita, but apparently was paid by town merchants, not the town itself. He was fired from that job; some say that Wyatt failed to share with other peacekeepers the bribes he received from town prostitutes. He showed up in Dodge City, Kansas, in 1878. He added to his reputation at the famous gunfight at the O.K. Corral while in Tombstone, where he was a silent partner in the Oriental Saloon, which is still in the Arizona town. If you're in town, stop in and toast Wyatt's memory. He'd like that.

After prospecting, unsuccessfully, for gold in Nevada, California, Idaho, and Alaska, Earp settled down in Southern California, where he lived out the final twenty-four years of his life. Wyatt dreamed of becoming a movie star, capitalizing on his legendary life as a gunfighter, but no one was interested in a senior citizen outlaw. He died peacefully in bed in Los Angeles in 1929, at age eighty-one.

So if you are challenged by Earp's gunfighting ghost, take it like a man. You couldn't outdraw him, and besides, his phantom bullets will do you no harm.

Vampire Cat Phantoms

The Manzanar National Historic Site sits just off State Route 395, between the small desert towns of Independence and Lone Pine. It is the only national historic site that commemorates a shameful incident in U.S. history—one that most Americans wish had never happened. Following the Japanese sneak attack on Pearl Harbor on December 7, 1941, Japanese Americans, most of whom lived in

California, were rounded up and moved into relocation camps in order to prevent any involvement in espionage or sabotage against America. This happened despite a lack of evidence of any widespread disloyalty among these people.

Manzanar was the first of ten internment camps established during the war, at one time containing more than ten thousand Japanese Americans. Closed by the end of World War II in 1945, the site now is eerily empty and desolate. All that remains is the stone entrance gate posts, the concrete guard posts, the former high school gym, now converted to a museum—and of course, the cemetery and the ghosts.

The cemetery is marked by a memorial tower that is inscribed, in Japanese characters, "Soul Consoling Tower. August 1943, erected by the Manzanar Japanese." The souls of those buried there apparently have been consoled and rest in peace. There are few reports of human spirits manifesting themselves here. Manzanar's ghosts are very different, very much in the Japanese tradition, and very scary.

Japanese folktales feature a legend about ghostly vampire cats. Now, those are three words you don't want to see together in one sentence; they are the stuff of nightmares. The ghosts of vampire cats are believed to contain all the fears and anxieties of people, and the relocated Japanese Americans surely were brimming with anxieties. The phantom vampire cats stalk the living, pouncing to gorge on fresh blood when their victim falls asleep. The only good news in this horrific scenario is that the ghosts of vampire cats always are solitary predators, like living cats, and will attack only solitary and sleeping humans. People in groups of two or more are safe, even if asleep.

So if you are near Manzanar, don't travel alone. And don't fall asleep.

The Shades of the Lost Jayhawkers

Death Valley earned its name during the winter of 1849–50 when dozens of men, women, and children died there. This tragedy was the result of an ill-advised search for a shortcut across this rugged, forbidding desert on the way to Los Angeles. These first recorded deaths in Death Valley produced some ghosts who, some say, still roam this savage land eternally searching for water.

An immigrant wagon train had set out from Salt Lake City in the early fall of 1849. Unlike the other forty-niners, who were heading for the goldfields of the Sierra, or to San Francisco, these immigrants were heading for the Los Angeles area with the intention of becoming farmers. The plan was to cross the driest, hottest part of the route in winter, when the heat would be least oppressive. July in Death Valley has produced temperatures as high as 134 degrees, the record for any place in the United States, so a winter crossing of this desert is the best choice. Even so, winter temperatures frequently exceed 90 degrees, and rain is a rare occurrence. Two inches of rain per year is typical. No wonder that the Native American name for Death Valley is *Tomesha*, "Ground Afire."

The ill-fated wagon train was following the Los Angeles–Salt Lake Trail, such as it was. It was poorly marked, and the only maps available were crude and often inaccurate. The wagonmaster was supposed to be an experienced guide, but some of the men traveling with the train had disagreements with the surly man and decided to find a shortcut across this forlorn wasteland.

A group of unmarried men calling themselves the Jayhawkers decided that they would travel faster by separating themselves from the slower wagons with baggage, women, and children aboard. They left the trail, which seemed to unnecessarily bypass the Panamint Mountains, in favor of following canyons through those mountains. But as they discovered repeatedly, these were "box canyons," which dead-ended in steep mountain rims where backtracking was their only option. Exhausted and running out of water, the Jayhawkers died by the dozen.

The wagon train that they abandoned fared little better, however. The group camped at Furnace Creek, waiting for scouts they sent ahead to return with water and food. Many were buried at Furnace Creek before being rescued. The survivors finally reached Los Angeles in March 1850.

The shades of the lost Jayhawkers are said to still stagger across Death Valley, searching vainly for that easy shortcut. The ghosts clutch at their dry throats as they wander aimlessly across the desert.

Don't worry, they won't approach you to ask directions; they're the Jayhawkers, disdainful of following the trail, and they're dead because of their stubborn ignorance.

Still on Patrol

A vacationing family from Los Angeles had an interesting encounter with what they believe was a ghost near Big Bear Lake. They are not sure exactly what happened; all they know is that a serious, potentially fatal accident was avoided.

Big Bear Lake, seven miles long, has become a major year-round resort center conveniently close to the Los Angeles metropolitan area. State Route 18 is also known locally as Rim of the World Drive, an appropriate name for a highway that is at times eight thousand feet above sea level. Enough snow falls in this vicinity to support a winter ski season.

The vacationing family, whom we'll call the Andersons, were following Rim of the World Drive along Big Bear Lake early on a wintry morning when, approaching a blind curve, they were flagged down by a lone highway patrolman. "Pull over here, off the road," he said. "There is a landslide just ahead." Doing as they were told, the Andersons pulled over onto the shoulder and put on their emergency flashers. Noticing that the patrolman was no longer in sight, the Andersons put out a flare on the road to warn other drivers. Within about twenty minutes, a few more vehicles had pulled over behind the Andersons.

Suddenly a loud, rumbling sound was heard, as though a freight train were passing nearby. The noise ceased as abruptly as it had begun, and a large cloud of dust billowed out from around the curve. Everyone exited their vehicles and walked cautiously around the bend in the road to see an amazing sight—the road was blocked by tons of rock debris.

When a highway patrol cruiser approached from behind the line of parked vehicles, the officer took one look at the landslide and told the group that they had narrowly escaped disaster. "How did you know to stop on this side of the curve?" he inquired. The Andersons told of their being flagged down by the first officer. "But where is he, and where is his patrol car?" queried the second officer. "No one else is scheduled for routine patrol in this sector." When the Andersons described the officer who had, they now realized, warned them of a landslide that had not yet happened, the officer told them, "That sounds just like Tom Higgins, but he passed away last week with a sudden heart attack."

Did the spirit of his recently deceased patrolman return to warn others of a landslide that he sensed was about to happen? The Andersons think so. It seems that officer Higgins was still on patrol to serve and protect.

Death Valley Scotty

The grizzled old-timer is the very picture of the Old West. His abundant facial hair is gray and picturesquely unkempt. Oddly, he is wearing a red tie with a bright blue shirt. Worn blue jeans, scuffed cowboy boots, and a big sombrero complete his outfit. He smiles and politely touches his hat brim in a salute to the ladies as he holds open the gate to the grounds of Scotty's Castle, a famous tourist attraction in Death Valley. As the party of tourists turns to thank him, they see nothing. The image of the old cowboy or prospector or whatever he was had evaporated, leaving behind only some dusty footprints. The visitors are unaware that they have just encountered the spirit of Walter E. Scott, better known as Death Valley Scotty, one of California's most memorable characters.

In life, Scotty worked hard at being a colorful character; in fact, he made a career and a good living out of typifying the sort of wildly independent, adventurous character that we like to envision as a true westerner. Walter Scott's life seemed to cover all the popular images of the Old West—cowboy, sharpshooter, bronco buster, gold prospector, and gunfighter. He was all of these, but he also was a clever showman and, very possibly, a likable fraud.

Scotty most probably was born in 1870. He gave various dates, depending on his mood. What is certain is that he died on January 5, 1954, after having lived an extraordinary life—at least to hear him tell it, which he did at every opportunity. It is true that he once drove the famous twenty-mule team wagons that carried borax out of Death Valley. He starred as a sharpshooter and bronco rider in Buffalo Bill's Wild West Show. There Scotty learned about image-building and public relations from the master showman, Buffalo Bill Cody.

Scotty decided that he would prospect for gold. Whether he actually found any is a good question, but he claimed to have discovered a rich mine somewhere in Death Valley. Once, on a business trip to Philadelphia, he claimed that a hundred pounds of gold nuggets had been stolen from his luggage. He got national publicity from that story, which not everyone believed. When visiting Los Angeles, he paid his bills with $100 bills and tipped lavishly. The "castle" that he built in Death Valley cost an estimated $2 million to construct in the 1920s. It actually was two houses connected by a patio, with a nearby guest house. The complex was cooled by an ingenious system of underground tunnels and pools. Many tourists taking the underground mysteries tour have claimed that Scotty's ghost appeared in the tunnels. Toward the end of his life, Scotty had led personal tours of his castle, always collecting cash for his time. When Scotty's wife sued him for divorce, it turned out that he had no assets at all. His castle had been financed by his good friend, a Chicago insurance company executive named Albert Johnson. The land it was built on was owned by the U.S. government as part of a national park.

Did Scotty in fact discover gold and spend the money living well, or was he a complete fraud who sold interests in his nonexistent mine? Certainly he was a public-relations genius who created an image the public wanted to believe: an eccentric millionaire who personified the Old West—a rugged, independent, and very colorful character. Just like his ghost, in fact.

Phantoms of the Caves

The haunted caves known as Mitchell Caverns are located about fifteen miles north of Exit 100 off I-40 between Needles and Ludlow. All the guidebooks and onsite signs warn visitors to enter only with a guide, and stay close to that guide. It would be easy to get lost in the vast labyrinth of underground chambers and passageways, but there is another reason, not often stated, to recommend a guide—the National Park Service, in charge of the Mojave National Preserve and the Mitchell Caverns National Preserve, just doesn't want any more mutilated bodies showing up. The paperwork alone that must document a tourist death is enough to bring tears to any bureaucrat's eyes, not to mention the horror of the decapitated, dismembered victims of the cave spirits.

Fortunately, a dead tourist's body hasn't been discovered for decades, but many are convinced that the evil spirits of the caverns are still trying to lure innocent victims deeper into the remote sections of the caves to murder them in the foulest, most gruesome manner demanded by ancient traditions of human sacrifices. The phantoms of Mitchell Caverns are a bloodthirsty lot, no doubt about it.

It would take at least three hours to walk across the cave complex, assuming you don't get lost. There are more than twenty entrances to the complex, which bears an abundance of signs of human habitation. Many of the walls and ceilings of the caves are covered with frescoes created by early cave dwellers. These frescoes often portray the wildlife of the area—jackrabbits, kangaroo rats, roadrunners, hawks, owls, coyotes, horned toads, and sidewinders, a type of small rattlesnake. Along with wildlife, however, some of these rock paintings show, in all their gory details, human sacrifice ceremonies. People, most likely enemy prisoners of war, may have been killed as offerings to the spirits who could lead the cave dwellers to game and to springs of sweet water.

The first white men in these parts quickly learned of the cavern's evil reputation. It was rumored that Michell Caverns not only had been long occupied by Indians, as evidenced by the frescoes and ashes from campfires, but were still occupied—by ghosts. Several early solitary explorers of the caverns were never seen again, at least alive. Coyotes sometimes were observed carrying large bones out of the caves—fresh bones that still had bloody flesh attached. On at least one occasion in the 1850s, it was claimed that a body was found deep inside the caverns, beheaded and gutted like a deer.

At dusk, as cool air rushes out of the cave to mix with warmer air, a strange moaning sound sometimes is heard. Is this a natural phenomenon caused by air expanding past the maze of pillars, stalactites, and stalagmites, or is it something more supernatural and sinister?

Could the spirits of those who died in Mitchell Caverns, whether of natural causes or as victims of ritual murder, be somehow trapped in the caves? Or are the spirits that allegedly infest the dark caves those of the ruthless murderers themselves? Perhaps we'll never know, but in the meantime, stay close to your guide if you visit these bloodsoaked caverns.

Metropolitan San Diego

METROPOLITAN SAN DIEGO, WHICH ALSO INCLUDES THE IMPERIAL Valley and lower Colorado Valley, runs down the Pacific coast from San Clemente south to the Mexican border, along the Mexican border to the Colorado River, and then along I-10 to San Bernardino and Ontario. Included in this region are the Salton Sea, Vallecito Mountains, and Chocolate Mountains.

In this region, you will encounter the ghosts of Spanish padres, stagecoach drivers, highwaymen, and some playful youngsters. The phantoms of a friendly cat and an aggressively protective rabbit make appearances, and a long-ago UFO shadows a stagecoach. A haunted house and a haunted hotel are major tourist destinations in San Diego. Enjoy your tour.

Phantoms of the Vallecito Stage

Down in San Diego County, State Route 78 across the Vallecito Mountains is noted in travel atlases as a scenic route, which indeed it is. To the east of the mountains is a rugged and rather forbidding desert, the area around the Salton Sea. This state highway follows an old stagecoach route that was pioneered by the famed Butterfield Stage, a prominent transportation company in its day. The Vallecito Stage Station was an important stop for the Butterfield Stages,

as it was located on a natural spring. It was a very welcome opportunity to water the horses and the people following a hot and thirsty trip across the desert.

The stage station, also known as Lassiter's Store, saw a lot of action back in stagecoach days. It is thought to be haunted by a variety of ghosts, including several gunfighters, stage drivers, passengers, and even a phantom horse—the infamous white stallion of Vallecito.

The story of the white horse begins with a stagecoach holdup. Robbers were so common along the stage routes that the Butterfield Stage operators advised every male passenger to equip himself with a Sharps repeating rifle and a thousand rounds of ammunition, as passengers were expected to help defend the stage during the almost certain attacks by mounted robbers.

On one trip, when the Butterfield Stage was carrying $65,000 in gold bullion, four robbers attacked the stagecoach. The driver managed to shoot one man. Another bandit was shot by his own partners, and the remaining two highwaymen escaped. They stopped to bury the loot on the way to the Vallecito Stage Station, where they proceeded to get very drunk. When the stage driver they'd robbed recognized them, they both jumped on a big white stallion, which took off like a rocket. Their corpses were found about a mile up the road. Apparently, they had shot each other in a dispute about the gold. To this day, it is said that a phantom white stallion, glowing with a greenish phosphorescence, charges past the stage station every midnight. Several people have tried to follow the ghostly horse, hoping it will lead them to the gold, but to no avail—the stallion is too swift, and the gold has never been found.

Another famous ghost is the White Lady of Vallecito. Her story is a tragic one. Her fiancé had left her in Baltimore to come to California and try his luck in the goldfields. He struck it rich and sent her the money to join him and get married. She bought a wedding dress and set out for San Diego by train and stage. Arriving at the Vallecito Stage Station exhausted and ill, she was carried from the coach into the station, where she died. Opening her luggage, the station operators discovered her wedding dress and dressed her in it for burial. To this day, the Lady in White's spirit wanders about in her wedding dress, the very picture of tragedy.

The Guest Who Never Checked Out

The Hotel del Coronado is a prominent landmark on Coronado Island, across the bay from downtown San Diego. Built in 1888, the historic hotel's unique red-peaked roof will seem somehow familiar to movie buffs. The hotel was prominently featured in the classic 1959 comedy *Some Like It Hot*, with Jack Lemmon, Tony Curtis, and Marilyn Monroe, when it was represented as a Florida resort. The del Coronado's reputation for unexcelled food in a classic Victorian ambience once led President Nixon to select it as the site of a meeting with the president of Mexico.

The Hotel del Coronado holds one more distinction: it hosts one of California's most famous ghosts. The hotel's staff will be glad to reserve any of its 688 units but will rent Room 3312 only on a special-request basis. Room 3312 is notorious for its ghost; some guests specifically request it, looking forward to a supernatural encounter, while the many non–ghost hunter guests who would prefer a good night's sleep stay in other rooms.

Pretty socialite Kate Morgan was a frequent guest at the del Coronado in its early days. When a passionate love affair went sour, despondent Kate committed suicide on the hotel's private beach in 1892. Supposedly, her ghost has chosen to haunt Room 3312, the room Kate would request for her rendezvous with her lover.

Room 3312 does not encourage a restful night's sleep. Kate Morgan is an equal-opportunity ghost—anyone, man, woman, or child, who stays in Room 3312 will have weird encounters with the supernatural. Lights in the room flick on and off with no human hand touching a switch. The television may or may not work, apparently depending on Kate Morgan's mood that night. Sometimes the TV screen remains blank whatever channel is selected, while agonizing loud screams issue from the speakers. The bathroom shower turns itself on or off at random. Once a male guest was shaving, looking at the mirror above the sink, when the face of a lovely young woman, tears streaming from her eyes, appeared in the mirror. He was quite alone—or at least, he thought he was.

At times the heavy sash window flies open suddenly, and a thick white mist fills the room even when the weather outside Room 3312 is clear and dry. The room temperature may drop abruptly to near freezing, then just as mysteriously return to normal. It is said that at least one guest in Room 3312 committed suicide within days after checking out. Maybe it would be best if you never check into Kate Morgan's room.

The Mysterious Passenger

The passenger railcar is described as "vintage," museum-speak for really old and interesting. This particular antique piece of rolling stock is on display and in occasional use at the Campo Railroad Museum, a short distance from the Mexican border east of San Diego. What is not always on display is the mysterious passenger who sometimes appears lounging on the worn leather seats at the back of the car.

One feature of the railroad museum is an opportunity to take a ninety-minute ride on an antique train through the dry backcountry of San Diego County. It is a great deal of fun, especially for kids. But watch out for the cowboy in the backseat—he is a ghost. This is not a particularly scary ghost. If approached too closely, he simply evaporates. Whoever he is, or was, he is the model of a polite gentleman. His ghost has been known to nod politely to any fellow passengers walking by his seat. He touches his hat brim to acknowledge ladies. If his car begins to fill up with tourists, he gives up his seat to the nearest lady—preferably a fine-looking younger lady— by simply disappearing.

No one seems to know why this phantom has chosen to haunt this particular vintage railcar. Some staff and regular riders and railroad buffs call him Sam but his real identity is a mystery. Some speculate that he was a regular passenger in a bygone era and still enjoys—as a spirit—a train ride in familiar surroundings. The railroad museum's staff claim that the mysterious passenger is a stickler for punctuality. If the train tour does not depart on time, the phantom pointedly pulls out an old-fashioned pocket watch and checks the time with a slight frown. But don't mind him, he never says a word to anyone, apparently preferring to simply look out the window and enjoy the ride. You should too.

The Spirit of the Friendly Cat

In life, Flake was not always a friendly or cuddly cat. Quite the opposite, in fact, for he was really half wild. As anyone familiar with cats will attest, they have distinctive personalities just as people have. And also like people, a cat's early environment has much to do with shaping its character.

The experience of one family in La Jolla, an upscale suburb of San Diego, suggests that a cat's personality can undergo a drastic change at the very end of its life, and that this change in attitude and behavior can persist after death in the spirit of the cat.

Flake was the younger of two cats in the household, junior to a big orange tom called Willie. Their histories and personalities were like day and night. Willie had been a gift from the older daughter's boyfriend and was named after him. He was a pampered pet from the moment he crossed the threshold, and he had an unusually friendly disposition. The family used to joke that Willie acted more like a puppy than a cat. Willie liked to curl up in someone's lap to nap and enjoyed attention from his human family. He was everyone's friend, a trusting and loving pet.

Flake came into the family under quite different circumstances. He had been found, half starved and with dirty matted fur, in a nest in the woods. No mother cat was in sight, perhaps the victim of a car on a nearby highway. Several kittens in the nest were dead; Flake was one of two survivors. This kitten was all black, which inspired his ironic name, Snowflake, which quickly was shortened to Flake.

Flake clearly was not used to being handled by people. He was distrustful and wary of humans, accepting food but not welcoming petting. Anyone insisting on picking him up and stroking him risked some nasty bites and scratches. Willie, gentleman that he was, accepted the appearance of a new kitten without hostility. As Flake matured, the two seemed to agree on a truce—they left each other alone and, in fact, ignored one another.

Willie was all friendly warmth and exercised due caution. Flake was standoffish and recklessly impulsive. It was a family joke that when the cats wanted to go out, someone would hold the door open while Willie looked outside cautiously and slowly advanced, one paw at a time, ever alert for danger. Flake, in contrast, would bound out the door in a blur, heedless of any possible danger. The family assumed that Flake would likely fall victim to a speeding car because of his reckless ways, but he always returned from his outdoor adventures, while it was cautious Willie who was killed in traffic.

When Flake was diagnosed with a fatal tumor by the vet, the family was devastated. They tried to comfort the obviously weakening cat, and to their surprise, Flake began to respond with feline affection, enjoying petting, even tummy rubs, and happily curling up in their laps to be stroked. It was as if Flake's lifetime habits of aloof independence and suspicion of humans had undergone a reversal. Flake was transformed by his final illness and the kindness of his human family into an affectionate and trusting pet.

When Flake was called to cat heaven, his family really missed him—but not for long. Each member of the family began having the same dream that Flake had visited them as they slept and nuzzled them playfully. Flake's ghost would rub up against their legs as they dozed off in front of the television set or would seem to jump into their laps. Were these little visits from the spirit of Flake or just dreams? Flake's family members are not sure, but they enjoy the affection of his spirit just the same.

Don't Disturb the Dead

The most famous haunted house in San Diego undoubtedly is the Whaley House. It is very much on the list of must-see list of visitors, whether or not they believe in ghosts. The Whaley House is located at 2482 San Diego Avenue in Old Town San Diego State Historic Park, a charming district of historic buildings, museums, restaurants, and boutiques. This Greek Revival two-story brick structure was built in 1856. It is said to be the oldest two-story house in California and at various times it has served as a residence, store, courthouse, and theater. It now showcases period interiors—and perhaps a few ghosts.

Visitors to the Whaley House will notice an unusual ticket-pricing policy: the price of admission goes up in the evening after 7 P.M. Why? Because more people prefer to visit at night, when ghosts sightings are more likely.

There aren't many rules about supernatural occurrences— ghosts, witches, and the like just don't seem to follow regulations by their very nature. But there are some common traditions, one being that disturbing the dead is likely to annoy their spirits, thus increasing the chances of a haunting. It is said that the Whaley House was built on the site of an old cemetery, not a good idea. Furthermore, the location once held a gallows for hanging condemned prisoners—another link with death.

One of those hanged here was "Yankee Jim" Robinson, who was convicted of stealing a boat. Yankee Jim's ghost is often seen rowing a skiff—inside the house! Other ghosts include those of Mr. and Mrs. Whaley, accompanied by the spirit of an infant. Many have reported not only seeing the Whaley family, but also smelling Mrs. Whaley's lavender perfume and her husband's cigar. The perfume smells better!

Other supernatural phenomena include furniture that levitates. Chairs, tables, and dining-room buffets rise slowly off the floor for no visible reason, then crash back down. Mysterious sounds include a crying baby and a barking dog, which never become visible. Enjoy your ghost tour.

Beware of the Attack Rabbit

This most unusual ghost is that of a former pet of an Oceanside family who did not wish to be identified. This is a nonthreatening spirit, at least to family and welcomed visitors, and it seldom puts in an appearance.

Pet rabbits normally are thought of as quiet, lovable, cuddly little companions, completely docile and people-friendly. They don't seem to have an aggressive cell in their furry bodies or attempt to bite, making them the ideal pet for children.

Powderpuff was an indoor rabbit. While many pet rabbits occupy an outdoor hutch, Powderpuff lived in a large cardboard box lined with newspapers and kept in the kitchen. She stayed in her box most of the time but occasionally left it to explore the house. Powderpuff could climb up the stairs, jumping from one step to the next, but had to be carried back down. The rabbit was everyone's friend. Even the family cat would curl up beside Powderpuff in her box for a nice nap together.

But then a home invasion changed everything. A thug, acting on a rumor that the family had a valuable coin collection, broke into the house. Unlike most burglars, who usually prefer to avoid confrontations, this invader burst in during the early evening and boldly and cruelly attacked the occupants, pistol-whipping the husband and abusing and raping the wife. The terrified cat wisely hid under a bed, but poor Powderpuff chose the wrong moment to bounce out of her box and come into the living room. In an act of unbelievable cruelty, the thug kicked the rabbit across the room into a stone fireplace. Powderpuff was sent to rabbit heaven by severe internal injuries.

The thug was captured by the police, who had been alerted by the neighbors that something very odd was happening. Press accounts of the brutal incident irresponsibly stressed that the would-be thief didn't find the coin collection, described as fabulous and featuring California-minted gold coins.

Inevitably, the allure of the well-advertised coin collection drew another greedy and reckless criminal to the house. This time it was different for the home invader, however, who soon was writhing in pain on the floor when discovered by the family. "That crazy rabbit attacked me!" moaned the culprit. "It jumped up and bit me!" Now, everyone familiar with rabbits knows that they can jump straight up in the air when startled or threatened. "Did it go for your throat?" asked one of the cops who responded to the emergency call. "Hell no!" was the answer. "The thing bit me in the crotch."

By now the police were openly laughing about the notion of a tough guy being bitten in a highly sensitive area by a rabbit. The cops really wanted to meet this courageous rabbit, but the husband told them, "We used to have a rabbit but it died. In fact, it was killed by the earlier crook."

The family is convinced that Powderpuff's ghost, outraged by attacks on its human family as well as itself, has undergone a radical change in personality. A family friend presented them with a homemade gift for their lawn, a sign saying, "Beware of Attack Rabbit," which sums up their belief. So far, the thought of long, sharp rabbit incisors in the groin has deterred more burglary attempts. The phantom of Powderpuff is on patrol!

The Shade of the High Roller

Once more frequently encountered, this benign, nonaggressive ghost now appears only rarely. This may be just as well, as this quiet phantom is frightening in a strange way—one that is related to the personality of the once-living man.

Travelers on the coast road between San Clemente and Oceanside pass through Camp Pendleton, the training base of the Marine Corps 1st Division. Much of this huge military base once belonged to a colorful character named Pio Pico, onetime governor of California, whose ghost has been reported along this stretch of coast.

Pio Pico lived to gamble. Born into a wealthy and influential family, he was able to indulge his passion for risk-taking frequently and on a grand scale. An enormous tract of land known locally as Rancho Santa Margarita once belonged to Mission San Luis Rey. When the Mexican congress secularized the missions between 1833 and 1837, these lands were returned to the local Indians. As is not uncommon today, political contacts can make the rich richer, and the Pico family had good connections. Pio Pico was a leader of the Californios, a group that had led a successful revolt against an unpopular dictatorial governor appointed in Mexico City without any input from the then-Mexican state of California.

Using their political clout, the Picos acquired more than 130,000 acres of Indian land near the Santa Margarita River. Pio bought out his brother's share of this huge ranch and purchased an additional 44,000 acres from Indian owners.

Pio Pico would bet on anything. He always carried a pack of cards and a pair of dice with him. It is said that when he rode far from home to attend horse races, he would bring along a mule loaded down with bags of silver coins with which to gamble. Pio was what modern casinos would call a high roller—happy to wager fortunes on cards, dice, horse races, or any game.

When Pio's ghost does materialize, he appears as a smiling, confident aristocrat, ready and eager to stake his wealth on any form of risk taking. The greater the risk, the broader his smile. Pio's gambling eventually caused him to lose his enormous ranch to his brother-in-law, a Yankee named John Forster, but Pio kept right on smiling—and gambling.

The smiling phantom of this high-roller should not be any cause for worry, because Pio Pico's ghost no doubt approves of the latest major gamble on part of what was once his ranch—the building of what is planned to be the nation's largest nuclear power generating plant. The San Onofre Plant of Southern California Edison and San Diego Gas and Electrical will be uncomfortably near one of California's many earthquake fault lines, and a major quake could produce a disaster—a gamble worthy of Pio Pico.

La Jolla Caves' Prankster Ghosts

The tourist feels a gentle tap on her shoulder from behind. Turning, she sees no one. She hears childish laughter, but there is no child in sight. Another visitor has the somewhat annoying experience of having a handful of sand poured down the back of his shirt collar as he kneels to examine an interesting seashell. Again, a light chuckle from an unseen child is heard as he expresses his displeasure. What is going on? Meet the prankster ghosts of the La Jolla Caves.

The seven La Jolla Caves are found in the base of the sea cliffs. Unlike most caves, such as Kentucky's Mammoth Cave or New Mexico's Carlsbad Caverns, which were produced by the erosion of limestone by underground water, La Jolla's caves are the result of the ocean's wave action. Carved from the base of sandstone cliffs, the La Jolla caves are open to the waves and daylight and are actually rather shallow.

The sharp contrasts of light and darkness, with constantly changing and shifting shadows, can play tricks on the eyes. Was that a fleeting glimpse of a child running or merely a shifting shadow caused by light reflecting off the surf? The crash of waves on the beach and into the foot of the caves creates sounds that are then distorted by the echoes within the caves. Was that the sound of a gleeful child or seagull's call? The caves are a magical small world of weird shadows and strange echoes. It is hard to be absolutely certain as to what one has seen or heard. The atmosphere is not spooky—there is too much natural light for that—but it is definitely different.

Some believe that the apparent pranks played on visitors—the tap on the shoulder, the pebble tossed, or the sand dribbled on people—are the jokes of ghostly children. The pranks are harmless—no one is ever injured or even really frightened. These minor annoyances are always accompanied by childish laughter. Have the spirits of deceased children decided to hang out at the La Jolla Caves to play practical jokes on visitors?

If you would like to see and hear these phenomena for yourself, the caves are accessible from Coast Boulevard. The easiest route is via a staircase from a souvenir shop at 1325 Coast Boulevard that leads to Sunny Jim Cave.

The Stagecoach and the UFO

The year was 1865. The Butterfield stagecoach was moving slowly up the long, steep pass across the mountains behind San Diego, as the four horses pulling it struggled against its weight. The driver was anxious to reach San Diego before nightfall, which was fast approaching. Dark rain clouds to the west blocked the sun on this winter afternoon. Traveling at night was an impossibility in the days before electric streetlights or headlights, so the stage had to make better time or be stranded in the wilderness.

The passengers, some of whom had come all the way from Salt Lake, were looking forward to a soft bed, a good meal, and a drink or two, having crossed the southern end of the Mojave Desert in a stuffy coach that rattled them like dice in a frantic gambler's hand. The horses plugged along, anticipating a rest in the cozy livery stable at their destination.

Suddenly a dazzling bright light from above broke through the gathering gloom. A huge disk, some one hundred feet in diameter, was slowly descending over the lumbering stagecoach, glowing, some said, like molten metal. Panic spread quickly among the people and horses alike. The horses, spooked by the sudden brilliance, put their hearts into dragging the stage uphill at a faster pace, not needing the whip wielded by the screaming driver. The four passengers each reacted in his or her own way. One young man decided to take action against the intruder, whatever it was. The stagecoach operators advised all male passengers to bring along a gun and plenty of ammunition, as the journey was beset by hostile Indians and ruthless highwaymen intent on robbery. The alarmed passenger accordingly leaned out the window and began firing his rifle at the hovering glowing craft, to no apparent effect. A middle-aged preacher among them launched into a lengthy impassioned prayer, which was joined by the young newlywed couple on their way to a new life together in California.

According to an account later recorded in the young wife's diary, the mysterious visitor shadowed the stage for a few minutes, then rose vertically and swiftly disappeared to the north, accelerating at an impossible speed. The passengers began discussing what had happened. The man who had fired upon the great disk was first to advance his theory. It was, he claimed, a "ghost sun," a magic replica of the sun created by an Indian shaman or medicine man, a supernatural object intended to frighten away the white men who were arriving in greater and greater numbers to take the Indians' land away from them. "What else could it be but magic?" he concluded.

The young woman, who was originally from coastal New England, reported that it was her family's tradition that "a ball of fire in the sky" had once circled a sailing ship off the Maine coast many years before. As in their own recent encounter, the unknown object had glowed with brilliant light and was capable of both hovering like a hawk and moving at fantastic speeds. Could both experiences describe the same weird object?

The preacher had an interesting interpretation, based, not surprisingly, on the Bible. The ancient Israelites, during their Babylonian captivity, had reported a fantastic image: a celestial object, traveling so quickly that it created a whirling sound in the heavens, appeared from a cloud, surrounded by flashes of lightning. It glowed like molten metal. The very strange creatures that came out of this fiery sphere also glowed with a bright light and could move with lightning speed. This description in the first chapter of Ezekiel, could possibly be interpreted as an encounter with a UFO, though the term unidentified flying object or UFO was not coined until the 1940s.

Did those aboard the stagecoach bound for San Diego on that fateful afternoon see what we would call a UFO? No one can ever know now, but there are many historical accounts that sound amazingly like UFOs.

According to Les Krantz in *America by the Numbers*, authorities receive about ten thousand reports each year from anxious Americans who claim to have spotted a UFO. More than twenty-five million people believe they had a close encounter of some kind, and according to a recent Roper poll, at least three million are convinced they have been abducted by aliens.

Auntie Rosa's Animal Advisors

A long-ago resident of San Diego had a reputation for being able to predict earthquakes—surely a vital gift in coastal California. Her neighbors thought that she was a witch, but was she?

She was known to all simply as Auntie Rosa; her complete name is lost to history. Rosa had an interesting profession for a witch, if indeed she was a witch. She ran a pet shop, offering a complete lineup of dogs, cats, birds, fish, rabbits, guinea pigs, even reptiles. Rosa had a reputation for never selling an unhealthy animal, and her establishment was always clean and cheerful. Rosa enjoyed matching up the appropriate pet with her observations of customer's personalities. With all of these positive attributes, why did some people think that she was a witch?

Rosa could predict earthquakes—or, more precisely, she could predict when one would strike in the vicinity of San Diego. She would tell all her friends and customers, never expecting any monetary rewards for her insight. At first those she told about an impending quake were quite skeptical. Everyone who was paying attention in San Diego, or anywhere along the California coast, for that matter, knew that sooner or later there would be a quake of some level of intensity. Minor tremors were frequent enough that people just rolled with them, quite literally.

Scientists could explain, and did so at irritatingly great length, exactly how and why earthquakes occur so commonly in California. The great cracks in the planet's solid crust, called fault lines, were mapped in detail decades ago. When one chunk of bedrock suddenly slips past another along the fault, an earthquake happens. Exactly where this slippage will occur along faults running for hundreds of miles cannot be predicted scientifically; neither can the timing of quakes be foretold. Except by Auntie Rosa, that is.

Rosa's reputation for accurate predictions of earthquakes led some to believe that she possessed supernatural powers—that she was a witch. How else could she know the unpredictable? The answer lay not in witchcraft, but in Rosa's close observation of her

animals. Scientists have at last acknowledged what many pet owners have known for years: cats, dogs, and horses behave strangely
in the days or hours before a strong quake. They get nervous and
skittish, sometimes refusing to lie down. The Japanese have also
observed the koi, or goldfish, kept in home aquariums become
tense, with their fins flared, just before a quake. How do the animals know? Do they somehow sense the tiny tremors that precede
a major jolt? No one really knows how they know that something
in the environment is wrong, but they do. Old Auntie Rosa was not
practicing witchcraft. She simply was watching her animal advisors
and friends.

So if you live in an earthquake hazard zone, pay attention to
your pets; they might be trying to tell you something.

The Cursed Orange Grove

Ask any agricultural expert about how a decision is made to grow a
particular crop on a specific piece of land, and you'll get a long lec-
ture. You start with the environmental characteristics required by
the plant being considered for cultivation. What kind of climate
and soil does it need to prosper and reward the landowner with
profits? Match the right crop to the climate and soil conditions, and
you'll have a successful operation. It seems so straightforward, but
as folks near Redlands discovered, it would be a good idea to first
check if the land is cursed.

Old-timers in the vicinity of Redlands claim that although the
area first grew as a navel orange shipping center, one small area
produced only misery and failure for would-be orange growers. The
story of the cursed orange grove begins in 1819, when the padres of
Mission San Gabriel established an outpost, the San Bernardino
asistencia, or chapel. After the Mexican congress secularized the
missions in 1842, the adobe chapel was abandoned, and the Mexican government granted the whole area to the Lugo family of Los
Angeles. The Lugos sold thirty-seven thousand acres to a colony of
Mormons who planned to go into the orange business.

The orange trees did well—except that is, on the spot of the
abandoned and destroyed chapel. While other groves in the neighborhood seemed to thrive, the trees on the site of the chapel did
not. Their blossoms died in frosts. They got root rot. They were

attacked by insects and diseases. They never produced a single orange, despite being surrounded by healthy groves.

In the late 1850s, an elderly Indian told of a medicine man's curse. He said that the padres had deliberately located the chapel on an ancient Indian burial ground, despite warnings from the local tribe. Indian protests were arrogantly ignored by the Spanish, who dismissed the locals' objections as mere superstition. The tribe's chief medicine man then placed a curse on this land—it would never support any that any non-Indians attempted, and indeed, the chapel did not function for long, and later efforts at orange growing on the spot failed as well. It seems that it's just not a good idea to ignore a curse.

Be Careful What You Ask For

Well, they can't say that they weren't warned. The warnings seem clear enough, at least to those who are attuned to the other world— the world of spirits. It just doesn't pay to disturb the dead.

The town of Temecula has prospered and grown quickly, thanks to I-15, which connects Los Angeles's eastern suburbs with metropolitan San Diego. A housing boom occurred here as the once-remote desert community was viewed as offering real estate bargains to those willing to undertake a long commute, either north to Los Angeles or south to San Diego.

It was the demand for housing that seems to have led to the latest supernatural defense of sacred graves. Temecula, which means "rising sun" in the local Indian dialect, was a sacred place to the Pala tribe. The "land of the rising sun" or the "bright land" was a favored spot for burials. This meant, to the Pala, that it was off-limits to the living as far as housing was concerned.

It is said that the Pala tried to explain this concept of avoidance of burial sites to white Americans arriving in the late nineteenth century, but to no avail. Temecula was chosen as the site of a railroad town when the railroad connecting San Bernardino and San Diego was built. The rails came through in 1882, and the town began to grow. "Not good," the Pala kept telling their new white neighbors. "Not good."

Despite the misgivings of the Pala, who were deeply concerned about building a town atop Indian graves, the town of Temecula grew. Its growth, however, worsened a problem already noted by its first arrivals. Water was in short supply. It looked as though the Santa Margarita River would be incapable of supplying enough water for the expanding town.

In desperation, Temecula's leaders approached the Pala Indians with a plea for help. Would the Pala be willing to entreat their spirits to produce some much-needed rain? Please? Some of the Pala people agreed to ask their dead ancestors to intervene with the gods of wind, clouds, and rain. It is said that their ancestors, still angry at the violation of their graves, decided to retaliate against the despoilers of their last resting place by giving the town what it asked for—but in unasked-for quantity.

It rained and rained and then rained some more. The torrential rains of 1892 washed out the railroad tracks, which were never rebuilt. Without its railroad service jobs, the town shrank to a population of only a few hundred.

Then came the interstate highway and the phenomenon of long-distance commuting. Once more, the population grew rapidly, threatening again to outgrow the local water supply.

There is talk among some Pala Indians as to whether the certain vengeance of the spirits whose graves became housing developments or shopping centers will produce another destructive flood, or their outrage will perhaps produce a long drought.

Maybe the town of Temecula shouldn't ask anyone to pray for rain. They might get it. Lots of it. Be careful what you ask for, if you've incurred the wrath of the dead.

The Ghost Galleon

The great galleon is under full sail as it seems to fly by. Its sails, marked by large red crosses, billow out as if driven on a strong wind, but there is little breeze. The banners of the ancient Spanish kingdoms of Castile and Aragon fly proudly from its mastheads. The high, ornately decorated stern carries the legend, *La Reina de España*, "The Queen of Spain." This sixteenth-century Spanish galleon is very much out of its own time in twenty-first century California, and considering that it is sighted near the southern end of the Imperial Valley's Salton Sea, the ship is very much out of place—a real ship of the desert.

The ghostly apparition of a majestic Spanish galleon improbably sailing across the desert has appeared repeatedly near Kane Springs, an old watering hole just off State Highway 78 north of Westmoreland. Old-timers in the neighborhood claim that it is the phantom of a Spanish galleon that got stranded here while searching for a water route between the Gulf of California and the Gulf of Mexico. No such water route exists, but the "Queen of Spain" allegedly was trying to find one. Supposedly, the galleon had sailed up a now-extinct arm of the sea, gotten stuck on a sandbar, and was slowly buried in sand dunes as the sea dried up. The galleon was said to be carrying tons of silver from the rich mines of Mexico.

Those few who have claimed to see the great galleon agree that it makes no sound as it glides past them, nor are any sailors in view. Is the phantom ship still seeking a channel to the sea?

An interesting footnote to the tale was an old prospector's claim to have stumbled across a large wooden hull half buried in a sand dune near Kane Springs. This was around 1890. The man's sincerity convinced the locals to go looking for the ship, which they found, then lost as a sandstorm covered it up once more. Some local historians say that, yes, they did find a wooden ship, but it was not the legendary "Queen of Spain," but rather a boat built in 1862 by a Colorado River mining company and hauled partway across the desert by mules before a steep mountain pass caused its abandonment.

Nonetheless, people still report glimpsing the mysterious galleon sailing across the desert on its endless journey back to the sea. Should you see it, follow it. Remember, it carried tons of silver treasure.

Guardians of the Highway

Many have had the experience, but only a few know that it was a supernatural one. Old-timers in this part of San Diego in the hills west of Mission San Diego Del Alcala like to tell the story of the man walking his dog. Now what could be more ordinary than a man out for a walk with his dog? The problem is that both the man and his dog are phantoms—they are not really there, except in the momentary perception of some drivers speeding on Mission Gorge Road or the smaller roads feeding into it.

The mystery of the ghostly man and dog is related to a tragic accident that occurred many decades ago. A car filled with teenagers was speeding recklessly through a particularly tight curve on the road. It was late on a winter evening, and a light rain was falling. Visibility was poor, the road was slick, and the driver was inexperienced, having just received his driver's license.

The sole survivor of the five friends celebrating the driver's successful driving test and brand new license told a harrowing tale. On a poorly lit curve, the driver suddenly spotted a man out walking his dog along the edge of the road. The roads in those days were narrower; the driver was afraid he might hit the man and dog, so he wrenched the steering wheel hard to the left. The car swerved suddenly into the opposing lane, sideswiped another car, and bounced back to the right. Before it soared off the cliff, it hit the dog and its master, killing them instantly. The other car hit an embankment, leading to two more fatalities.

This horrendous accident contributed to a major widening effort on the road. It also produced the ghostly dog walker and dog, who seem to patrol that stretch of highway. These phantoms appear when a vehicle is taking the curves too fast. The misty, slightly phosphorescent forms appear far enough ahead of the speeding car, apparently ambling along the side of the road, that the driver has time to slow down without risk of losing control.

Are the man and dog ghosts trying to prevent a repeat of the type of accident that took so many lives? Many drivers on that hazardous road think so. Perhaps the spirits of the man and his dog have somehow adopted that road as their opportunity to help prevent more senseless deaths. These are classic "guardian ghosts"— trying to warn the living of dangers that could send them into the spirit realm.

San Joaquin Valley

CALIFORNIA IS THE MOST PRODUCTIVE AGRICULTURAL STATE IN THE United States in terms of both the value and variety of its crops. The San Joaquin Valley, which lies between the Coast Ranges to the west and the Sierra to the east, and stretches from Los Banos and Chowchilla to Lancaster and Palmdale, is the main contributor to the state's top rank and includes a high percentage of the country's irrigated land. Along with its crops, the San Joaquin Valley produces a large and varied array of tales of supernatural phenomena. Traditional Spanish witches appear, as do the spirits of a charming grandmother, a cranky recluse, and a helpful schoolteacher. The phantoms of the valley also include a highwayman who literally lost his head and a band of African camels.

Playing Hide and Seek with Ghosts

The landscape is especially rugged around Soledad Gorge in the San Gabriel Mountains, which form the northern edge of the Los Angeles Basin. This forested wilderness constitutes a stout barrier to the further northward spread of the metropolitan area. The jumbled rock formations create a kind of natural maze in which it is easy to get lost. Beyond the area of tilted blocks of solid rock are the Vasquez Caves, a series of shallow caves formed by wind and rain erosion, unlike most caves, which are made by underground water slowly dissolving limestone.

This fantastic landscape of jumbled blocks of sandstone backed by an intricate network of caves is said to be haunted. The ghosts of the bandit Tiburcio Vasquez and his gang have been seen here for more than 140 years. Vasquez and his band of thugs terrorized the area in the 1860s. The Vasquez gang seemed invincible. They boldly robbed banks, merchants, ranchers, and stagecoaches before retreating to their hideout in the caves. Time after time, pursuing lawmen lost sight of the bandits as they made their way through the natural maze of rock blocks. Every time, Vasquez and his men were able to escape their pursuers and take refuge in the caves. But at long last, the secrets of the tortuous pathways through the rocks were revealed—by a trail of blood.

Vasquez had shed a great deal of innocent blood over the years. His raids on towns and ranches left behind many dead and wounded victims of his ruthless greed. At long last, however, it was Vasquez who sat bleeding in his saddle, severely wounded by a sheriff's bullet as the gang fled an unsuccessful bank robbery.

The notorious bandit's lifeblood oozed from his wounds, leaving a trail that the lawmen could follow like a road map. This time, they followed the gang right back to their no-longer-secret hideout. The Vasquez gang fought its last gun battle in the caves, and every outlaw died that day.

It is said that the ghosts of Vasquez and his band of thugs still move slowly through the rocks, trying in vain to erase the blood trail that would betray their hiding places. But try as they might, the bloodstains persist. Justice would catch up with them at last, and death would descend swiftly. Their spirits are condemned to try to rub out the blood, but in this case, blood will tell. The brutal game of hide-and-seek is over.

The Headless Robin Hood

In life, Joaquin Murrieta was a very controversial, but always interesting, character. To the Mexicans who found themselves living under American rule after the 1846–48 war between the United States and Mexico, he was a hero. When Yankee gold miners mistreated Mexicans in what had been Mexican land, Murrieta intervened, violently. To the newly arrived Americans, Murrieta was nothing more than a bandit who specialized in robbing stage-coaches throughout the San Joaquin Valley and the gold camps in the Sierra foothills.

Murrieta had a brief but colorful history as an outlaw. Some-times called the "Mexican Robin Hood," he began his career as a robber of Yankees and friend to poor Mexicans in 1851. He was tracked down and killed by an American posse in July 1853.

Gold was the big reason that California became part of the United States rather than Mexico's northwestern state. The discov-ery of gold attracted an avalanche of Yankees, who quickly out-numbered the Mexican ranchers. There was a racist element in the disdainful treatment of Mexicans by the Yankee miners and adven-turers. Joaquin Murrieta began giving a portion of his loot to poor Mexicans, who saw an ironic justice in sharing the proceeds of armed robbery victimizing the hated Yankees. As a result, Murrieta was afforded sanctuary in Mexican communities, making it difficult for the law to bring the notorious bandit to justice.

The Mexican Robin Hood contributed to his own legend with his fearless attitude and sense of humor. Once, riding into a small town, he spotted a poster offering a $1,000 reward for his capture. He dismounted, went up to the poster, and in front of a crowd of onlookers, wrote, "I'll give $10,000!" and signed his name. The townspeople laughed, applauded, and let him leave without a shot fired.

Another time, he ventured north of his usual territory to Mokelumne Hill and went into the famed Zumwalt Saloon, a hang-out of gold miners, assorted desperadoes, cowboys, and ladies of the evening. Unrecognized, Murrieta sat peacefully playing cards. The talk got around to the Mexican Robin Hood and a young miner who'd had too much to drink slapped a leather bag of gold dust on the bar and loudly proclaimed, "Here's $500 that says I will kill that SOB!" Leaping up on the bar, a pistol in each hand, Murrieta said, "I am Murrieta. Now is your chance!" No one moved. Murrieta took the bag of gold and left. No one got in his way.

The little town of Priest Valley, near Coalinga, was where the Mexican Robin Hood made his last stand. The state had posted a $5,000 reward for him, dead or alive. Murrieta's former wife told the sheriff where her onetime husband liked to hide out, and a posse of twenty-one gunfighters tracked him down. Murrieta's longtime lieutenant, called Three-Fingered Jack, was killed first, followed by the Mexican Robin Hood himself. The victorious posse's chief, Captain Love, cut off Murrieta's head and packed it in salt, along with Three-Fingered Jack's disfigured hand, to prove his claim to the reward. The preserved head and hand then went on tour around the state, where citizens paid a dime to view the grisly relics.

Murrieta's head and Three-Fingered Jack's hand both disappeared in San Francisco during the 1906 earthquake. No one, apparently including Murrieta's ghost, knows where the head might be, but it is said that he is still wandering about looking for it. Murrieta's headless ghost is unlikely to ever locate the head, and it's probably a good idea to stay out of his way, as he's kind of cranky about being beheaded.

The Camels of Fort Tejon

A dozen or so camels plod silently across the dry hills, looking like a common scene out of the Middle East. But this is not anywhere in the Middle East; it is Southern California, and the awkward-looking beasts are very much out of place. They also are very much out of their own time, for these are the ghosts of camels past. Their trek through the Tehachapi Mountains actually did happen in the middle of the nineteenth century, ending here at old Fort Tejon.

The sight of either the real camels or their phantoms in California must have caused wonder and disbelief among onlookers then and now. A glimpse of the ungainly "ships of the desert" is said to have startled early Californians to the extent that drunks witnessing the sight even swore off drinking, sometimes for whole days.

It is a matter of historical record that camel trains did arrive at Fort Tejon in 1858 and departed the following year. Fort Tejon had been established by the U.S. Army in 1854 to protect travelers from highwaymen and maintain the peace with the local Indians. It was located in a mountain pass on the road between Bakersfield in the San Joaquin Valley and Los Angeles, nestled in its coastal basin. The U.S. Army's experiment with the use of camels was an imaginative attempt to provide suitable beasts of burden for Army operations in the deserts of the Southwest. The thinking was that since

camels are perfectly suited to travel across the Sahara, they would work well in places like Arizona and California's Mojave Desert.

But Operation Camel was a failure because of two problems. The large pads of the camels' feet, adapted to the soft sands of their homelands, were not suited to the sharp rocks more typical of southwestern American deserts. Also, camels are not as easy to manage as horses or burros. Camels make the most stubborn and ornery mules seem like puppies. They are every bit as independent minded as alley cats, and they don't hesitate to bite. They also are champion spitters, able to spit foul-smelling saliva with great accuracy.

The U.S. Army surrendered to camel orneriness (and their sore feet) in 1864 and auctioned them off to anyone stupid enough to buy one. When the Army ran out of people who (a) had some money and (b) didn't know much about camels, they turned the survivors loose. For years afterward, stray camels scared the devil out of travelers and cowboys, until they finally died.

To this day, the immaterial shades of camels past are said to haunt the Tehachapi Mountains, walking in single file and looking like a biblical scene, so out of place in California. Watch out—they spit.

The Phantom Dancers of Devils Den

Looking like eerily phosphorescent clouds of mist, the phantom dancers circle the fire pit. The dancers seem to weave about in slow, random patterns, staggering as if they were very drunk. But it is not alcohol that explains their uncoordinated stumbling; it is their use of a powerful narcotic drug. These ghosts are continuing in the spirit world what some California Indians did many centuries ago—they are high on jimsonweed and are reenacting a religious ceremony.

The Toloache cult was especially popular in the San Joaquin Valley at the time of the European discovery. Toloache was centered on the use of jimsonweed to induce hallucinations. The local Indians believed that the weird images and exotic dreams that resulted from using jimsonweed put them in touch with the spirit world. Deeply under the influence of the drug, people thought that they could communicate with deceased relatives and friends.

First the adherents of Toloache would create a large sand painting, using different-colored sands to represent the present world.

Then they would consume jimsonweed and wait for it to take effect. Under the drug's influence, the dance would begin. After hours of seemingly aimless dancing on and through the sand painting, the exhausted dancers would collapse and sleep off the drug. When they awakened, they would examine the deranged sand painting and interpret its meaning, believing that the new patterns created by their dancing feet revealed the future.

The ceremonial dance under the influence of narcotics could not be performed just any place. The venue had to be sacred—a place where their ancestors had danced for centuries. One such place is Devils Den, about fifty miles northwest of Bakersfield. There are several stories of how Devils Den got its name, but one is that early European settlers were spooked by the activities of the ghostly dancers of Toloache.

To this day, some claim that late at night when there is no moonlight, the spirits of the Toloache dancers can be seen as shadows weaving erratically around the campfire in a deserted part of the countryside. It definitely is not a good idea to approach them. And by the way, do not be tempted to try using some jimsonweed yourself—it is highly toxic and could make you into a ghost too.

Legend of the Weeping Woman

She has been seen along the rivers of Southern California, but most frequently on the banks of the San Joaquin River and the many streams feeding into it—the ghostly figure at once both pathetic and frightening, of a beautiful woman wearing a long, white gown. As told in centuries-old Spanish folklore, this phantom is La Llorona, the weeping woman, and she is both to be pitied and to be feared. La Llorona's long black hair frames a tragic, tear-stained face. Her pathetic wails can be heard in the distance even before her misty figure comes into view.

The infamous weeping woman appears differently to adults than to children. She is the picture of desolation and despair to adults, as she weeps and wails in anguish at the drowning deaths of her children in the river she patrols. But to children, she is a smiling, encouraging mother figure, luring them closer and closer to her with promises of treats. When unwary, trusting children get close enough,

La Llorona grabs them and heartlessly drags them down to a watery grave, for she ruthlessly drowns children. The figure in white is said to laugh in triumph as another child sinks below the water.

There are several versions of why the weeping woman is a serial killer. One story is that she was witness to the accidental drowning of her own children, and the tragedy unhinged her mind. When priests and friends trying to comfort her in her terrible grief told her reassuringly that her offspring now were in a better place, La Llorona embarked on a demented mission to send other children to paradise as well.

In another variation of the legend, the weeping woman is self-ishly mourning the loss of her immortal soul. She made a pact with the Devil. In order to achieve immortality as a beautiful woman's phantom, she deliberately murdered her own children by throwing them in a river to drown. Now her spirit is condemned to wander along riverbanks looking for more children to toss into their watery graves.

So look out for the weeping woman. She constantly seeks new young victims of the curse of La Llorona.

The Witches of Visalia

Visalia is notable for being the oldest city between San Francisco and Los Angeles, having been founded in 1852. It is known as the gateway to the very popular Sequoia and Kings Canyon National Parks. Visalia also is famous for its witches.

Las Brujas, to give them their original Spanish name, are infa-mous not only for terrorizing people, but also for fighting among themselves. Las Brujas have been seen in the vicinity of Visalia since before the city was founded. The witches have been known to appear almost anywhere in this charming, prosperous city. Most recent sightings have taken place in and around Mooney Grove Park, south of downtown, so you've been warned. Traditional satanic ceremonies are most frequently carried out by witches on nights with full moons.

Las Brujas build an open fire just before midnight. Some people claim that these Spanish-heritage witches don't need matches to start a fire—they just point with their index fingers. As the fire grows, the witches begin to dance about it, starting slowly and then increasing in momentum. As the dance becomes more frantic, a figure appears to rise from the flames—Satan himself. The Prince of Darkness appears, summoned by the witches' dance, to choose a new lover from among them.

Any person observing this must remain well hidden, as detection could lead to a very painful death. The witches present now begin to compete with one another for their evil master's attentions. At this point, the dance becomes truly obscene, with X-rated gestures and contortions. One by one, all but two witches collapse, exhausted by the dance and ignored by Satan, whose eyes are on the two finalists vying for his favor.

The last two witches are caught up in a whirlwind and transform into balls of fire, twirling like old-fashioned pinwheel fireworks. The two dueling fireballs rise up in the night air, spinning faster and faster, repeatedly diving at each other like dogfighting fighter planes.

Finally, one triumphs over the other. The loser falls back to earth as a rain of cinders; the winner merges with Satan above the flames of the dying fire. The dance of Las Brujas is over, at least until midnight of the next full moon.

Please Help Me!

The house sits on a side street in a residential neighborhood near the California State University in Fresno. It is a very ordinary-looking house, a bit run-down in appearance. A general air of neglect has settled over the structure; it is the kind of property that real estate salespeople would describe as one that "needs tender loving care." This old house is unlikely to get much care, though, as each new owner quickly comes to regret buying it. The house is haunted.

The big, old place is carved up into a handful of small apartments that are duly advertised as available to students at the nearby university. Each September, a new crop of unsuspecting students signs leases, assuming that the very reasonable rent reflects the somewhat shabby appearance. They soon learn better. They seldom stay in the house more than a few weeks.

As is common in haunted house stories, new occupants notice nothing strange at first; the spirit or spirits don't make an immediate appearance. Then it begins. A child's whimpering cry is heard late at night. Sometimes a thudding, thumping sound is heard on the stairs, as though someone had lost their balance and fell. Pathetic screams of a child awaken the residents, but no one is there—no one living, that is. More than one short-term occupant has been awakened in the middle of the night by someone or something leaning over him or her in bed and whispering, "Please help me!" The tear-stained face of a young girl has been seen from the street at an upstairs window, apparently trying to call for help.

Neighbors familiar with the house believe that the pathetic little ghost, pleading for help, is that of a child who died there in mysterious circumstances. The girl was killed in a fall down the stairs. Was it an accident, a suicide, or a murder? It had been rumored that the young girl was being shamefully abused by her uncle, with whom she lived. And so her ghost endlessly relives her torment and violent death. "Help me, please help me!" begs her spirit.

This house is on the market almost every year. Looking for a cheap investment property?

Haunted Underground Gardens

Forestiere Underground Gardens is a unique tourist attraction located about three miles east of downtown Fresno. The underground garden complex is a maze of subterranean rooms, galleries, passageways, gardens, patios, and courtyards, all connected by tunnels and illuminated by skylights. This fantastic construction has been compared to the famous catacombs of Rome, with similar masonry work and stone arches. The sprawling underground network contains a home and a charming little chapel. Forestiere Underground Gardens is very interesting, even without its resident ghost adding to the appeal.

This wonderful subterranean world was the life work of one man, Sicilian immigrant Baldasare Forestiere, who devoted four decades to its creation. Most people have an urge to create, express themselves, and develop their talents and skills. A special few are driven to devote many years to their dreams of leaving a unique mark on the world, a dazzling achievement that will stand out in the landscape. The Forestiere Underground Gardens are not California's only such monument to individual creativity. Los Angeles's Rodia Towers are a better-known example of this compulsion to create landmarks. These three metal and concrete structures, decorated with bits of china and glass, were built by tile setter Simon Rodia between 1921 and 1954. Whereas Baldasare Forestiere built down, Simon Rodia built up—his tallest tower is one hundred feet in the air over the Watts section of L.A.

It is said that the ghost of Baldasare Forestiere haunts his underground gardens, but his ghost is friendly and unobtrusive. Forestiere's spirit is said to tag along with groups taking the guided tour. The elderly gentleman is dressed conservatively in an old-fashioned, dark three-piece suit. His barrel-like torso and powerful arms testify to a lifetime of hard physical labor. He follows the tour group at a slight distance, smiling broadly as the guide enthuses about the beauty and craftsmanship of the underground garden complex. The phantom will nod politely if any tourists look his way but never utters a sound, before seeming to disappear around a corner or pillar. It would seem that the ghost of Baldasare Forestiere is simply enjoying his daily tour of his creation, taking justifiable pride in his accomplishment. Few have left such a remarkable mark on the world—he deserves to be proud.

Be Polite to the Ghosts

Bakersfield's Highland High School is haunted—or more precisely, its theater-auditorium is haunted. Two ghosts have been seen to manifest in the backstage area.

The more active phantom is that of a middle-aged man; the other is the spirit of a teenage girl. The ghostly man is thought to be that of a former teacher at the school named Philip Mason. Mr. Mason is said to have joined the faculty when it opened and stayed for thirty years as an English teacher and drama coach who enjoyed directing student plays and musicals. Supposedly, Mason's spirit never left. The second ghost is that of a teenage girl, known only as Mary Jane, who fell to her death on the stage. She had gone up on the narrow catwalks high above the stage to reposition a spotlight, lost her balance, and plunged headfirst to her doom.

In life, Philip Mason was the kind of teacher that we all wish we had in every class. He put in long hours working with his students, encouraging them to do their best as actors, stagehands, props coordinators, scenery painters, lighting and sound technicians—everyone involved in putting on plays. Rehearsals and preparations meant that he didn't leave the building until late in the evenings on many occasions. Although his students regarded him as a friend, Philip Mason liked to maintain his status and authority and required his students to always address him as sir. "Goodnight, sir" was the formal goodbye as students finished evening preparations and rehearsals. Anyone who forgot earned a steely glare from Mr. Mason.

After Mason's death, it became a Highland High tradition that on leaving the stage area, everyone would say, "Goodnight, sir," to the empty backstage. Each new class of students began to realize that, in fact, failure to thus politely acknowledge Mr. Mason's spirit would be punished in some small way—key props would disappear overnight, scenery would be shredded. Philip Mason's ghost is said to appear backstage just before or during showtime for student plays. More than one student actor swears that a ghostly voice whispered the next line to them if they forgot while onstage.

As for the other ghostly presence, Mary Jane, it was discovered that she too demanded appropriate recognition. Students learned to say, "Thank you, Mary Jane," when leaving the backstage. If that small courtesy was omitted, lights would turn themselves on or off at the wrong times. Spotlights would flicker mysteriously, and on occasion, heavy overhead lights crashed to the floor.

It seems that both spirits are intent on teaching manners to students, which is not at all a bad thing. After hours, say "Good night, sir," and "Thank you, Mary Jane," to ensure that no pranks or accidents occur. You can't be too careful, or too polite.

Don't Mess with Uncle Carlos

Uncle Carlos has been dead for over forty years now, but some parents around Fresno still warn their misbehaving children, "Watch out or Uncle Carlos will get you!" Old Uncle Carlos (no one knew his full name) lived by himself on a small farm on the edge of town. His wife dead and his children elsewhere, he subsisted on Social Security checks and grew most of his own food in a large garden. He kept some chickens and a goat or two and "lived small," as he put it. As he grew older and crankier, he began to get a reputation in the neighborhood as a grouchy recluse. The local kids started to harass him just to see him rage at them.

One of Uncle Carlos's eccentricities was that he firmly believed in the supernatural. To him, ghosts, witches, vampires, monsters, and UFOs were unquestionably real. Whatever misfortune might befall him was undoubtedly the work of witches. Did his tomato crop get attacked by insects? Witchcraft! Did his hens stop laying eggs? An evil spell had been cast on them! Did his roof develop a leak? It must have been the death rays aimed at him from UFOs. Uncle Carlos would warn the kids who tormented him that ghosts and witches would make their lives miserable in retaliation. They just laughed—until after Uncle Carlos went to his eternal reward, that is. But things changed around the neighborhood following Uncle Carlos's burial.

The leader of the gang who had made life miserable for Uncle Carlos was the first to experience ghostly wrath. An unseen hand poked a broomstick through the spokes of his speeding bicycle, resulting in a wrecked bike and some nasty cuts and abrasions. Next, he claimed, Uncle Carlos's spirit broke into his bedroom at night, tossed a few snakes onto his bed, and laughed at the boy's panic.

Then the other boys who had participated in harassing Uncle Carlos began to suffer a series of mysterious accidents. One swore that Uncle Carlos materialized in front of him and threw him into a deep mud puddle. Later that evening, someone or something tossed an agitated skunk into his family's house, with predictable results.

Another naughty member of the gang was abducted, he swore, by a large sweaty man who looked exactly like Uncle Carlos. The man carried him for a terrifying mile before releasing him unharmed. Later, his normally calm, sweet-natured dog turned on him and inflicted some serious bites before being pulled off.

Then the specter of Uncle Carlos began stalking his former tormentors. Just the sight of his phantom would send the boys running in terror. As all the neighborhood parents began to warn, "Be good or Uncle Carlos will get you!"

The Ghost's Menagerie

This experience was related by a family in Bakersfield on the grounds of anonymity. This is a ghost story, but this ghost is not particularly scary. Far from it! The ghost is sympathetic, rather likable in fact.

Mama Yanuzzi (not her real name) was the matriarch of a large Italian American family. She much enjoyed being a mother and grandmother; nothing made her happier than hosting the whole family at holiday dinners. Mama was a superb cook; her marinara sauce was legendary. Normally she was very easygoing and tolerant of childish pranks and roughhouse play, except for one sensitive area. Over the years, she had acquired, mostly as gifts, a collection of little animal figurines, made of glass, pottery, wood, plastic, stuffed cloth, even carved stone. It had grown to a menagerie of tiny animals. Whimsically, Mama segregated the figurines on different bookcases. Predators, like lions, tigers, bears, and alligators, were kept in what Mama termed the "fierce corner," while creatures like rabbits, dogs, giraffes, horses, and kangaroos were assigned to the opposite "gentle corner."

It was understood that visiting children were permitted to handle her figurines gently, but they must always put them back where they belonged. Mama was adamant about this, and her seldom-seen temper could flare if they ignored this rule.

In the course of time, Mama was promoted to heaven, and a family conference determined that rather than sell her house immediately to divide up her estate, the house would be rented to Mama's favorite granddaughter, recently married. The granddaughter and her husband moved into Mama's fully furnished house, needing to bring only their clothing and personal effects.

Soon after moving in, the young couple began to sense the benign presence of Mama's spirit. The delightful aromas of Mama's cooking and baking would waft in from an empty kitchen in which no food was currently being prepared. Occasionally Mama's favorite operatic arias could be heard playing softly on her CD player, even if it was unplugged.

It was when the little animals in Mama's collection were moved, however, that Mama's spirit began to make itself known more forcefully. When the granddaughter decided that the figurine collection was a dust collector of little interest to her, she carefully wrapped and packed them away in a box in the attic. The following morning, the animals of the collection had been restored to their accustomed places. Now that got the young couple's attention. As a test, the husband deliberately moved a little glass lion to the "gentle corner"—a provocative sacrilege to Mama. The very next time the husband and wife entered the room, the lion was back in its assigned place among the other fierce creatures.

The newlyweds decided, wisely, that as long as they lived in Mama's house, the collection would remain untouched. After that the figurines rested peacefully, as did Mama's spirit.

The Shape-Shifting Witch of Tulare

Are there really witches, or are those accused of witchcraft merely misjudged, lonely old women? In retrospect, the supposed witches who were burned at the stake in colonial New England probably were innocent of any evil intentions or supernatural activities. They may have been cranky recluses, but it was never proven, in the case of the Salem witches, that those hapless women really were in league with Satan.

Nonetheless, a significant number of people believe in witchcraft and witches. Some even proclaim that they are, in fact, witches. How would you know a witch if you saw one? A century ago, an alleged witch, one Tabitha Watson, lived in the small city of Tulare.

Tabby, as her neighbors called her behind her back, may well have been a witch, or at least an old lady who encouraged the suspicion that she was a witch. She lived alone, in a rather gloomy old house on the edge of town. She most definitely did not welcome visitors, so the local belief that she was a witch could have been an asset in preserving her privacy. Tabitha had never married and never held a job. Her late parents had been poor, but she never seemed to lack money. Tabby always paid her bills in local shops with gold or silver coins. A rumor started that hidden in her somewhat ramshackle house was a large sack of gold and silver, earned by casting spells and secretly selling magical potions.

A couple of local thugs decided to rob Tabitha of her silver and gold. Late one evening, they carefully crept up to her house. Peering through the windows, they saw no sign of the old lady and decided to enter her house. But as they opened the door, the would-be burglars were confronted by a large black cat. The cat arched its back, elevated its tail, and hissed at them, its yellow eyes brimming with malice. When the thugs froze on the spot, the cat attacked.

Claws and teeth ripped at their faces and shredded their clothing. One robber managed to strike the cat above its left eye, causing an open wound, but not perceptibly slowing the whirlwind of fangs and claws. The two men ran off as fast as they could.

Curiously, when Tabitha next visited the store for her weekly order, people noticed that she had a fresh scar above her left eye, exactly where the cat had been wounded, according to the thugs' talkative drinking companions. Had Tabitha transformed herself into an aggressive cat to defend her money? No one can be sure, but traditional powers of witches include "shape shifting," the ability to take the form of another creature, such as a bat, wolf, or cat.

Following the abortive attempt to rob her, people learned to leave Tabitha—and her cat—strictly alone. She lived a long if somewhat lonely life. When at last Tabitha died, no one could find any trace of her cat.

The Pact of the Twins

Family members related this strange tale on the understanding of anonymity. This event took place a generation ago in a quiet neighborhood of Fresno.

It is widely known that twins have a special bond between them. This is especially true of identical twins, which Samantha and Susanna were. Not only did they look exactly alike, but their talents and interests matched perfectly as well. Sam and Sue, as they called each other, were both accomplished piano players, and both were interested in the supernatural.

In the course of time, Sam and Sue each married, bore several children, and pursued the same career as schoolteachers. As they aged, their mutual interests in the occult led to lengthy discussions of the possibility of communication between the living and the dead. Was it possible for a deceased loved one to send a message from the spirit world to a living person?

The twins were well aware that many self-proclaimed mediums were frauds, so they agreed that whichever sister died first, she would attempt to contact the survivor directly, not through any intermediary. They chose a secret code word, "violets," to identify their phantom communications, so that no one else could fake a message from the spirit world. By now, both were widows.

Samantha, who coincidentally had been born first, died first. Days before her passing, the twins reaffirmed their secret pact. "Violets" would be mentioned in any message.

Following Samantha's voyage into the world of the dead, Susanna waited with great interest for any contact from her twin. Weeks, then months passed without a word. Sadly, Sue had to accept that she might never again speak with her beloved sister. Perhaps the dead really could not communicate with the living after all.

Then one day a frantic Susanna called each of her children to her home. "Samantha has come for me," she announced. "She has come to escort me into the spirit world. I was half asleep when Sam entered my room. She seemed to float above the floor. Smiling, the ghost of Samantha said, 'Violets, my dear sister, violets—have no fear, but before midnight this day you will join me in a world of peace and light.' With that, the image faded away." And sure enough, Susanna went to join her twin just before midnight. Sue died with calm look of anticipation on her face as she envisioned a reunion with her twin.

Did Samantha really reach across the spiritual barrier to deliver a reassuring message to her twin about to die? Or did Susanna have a premonition of death and dream about her sister? Her family is divided on exactly what happened, but clearly something unexplainable had given Susanna advance notice of impending death.

The Enchanted Cane

The curious case of the enchanted cane is reported by a Fresno family whom we'll call the Beams. This particular cane became a part of the household when the family matriarch, Gran, had hip replacement surgery. Gran (she preferred being called Gran rather than Granny, which she thought made her sound older) had ruled benevolently over her large family for years. While she might have been seen by some as a meddlesome old woman, she had everyone's interests at heart. The advice that she freely pressed on her family members almost always turned out to be very sound. Her lavish gifts on holidays and birthdays were legendary and much appreciated. A retired schoolteacher, Gran provided plenty of encouragement along with help with school projects and homework for children, grandchildren, and great-grandchildren in turn.

Inevitably, Gran herself needed help. A hip replacement operation made her very dependent on her youngest daughter and her family, with whom Gran lived. When Gran graduated from a walker to the use of a cane, the family was introduced to the cane that would eventually prove to be a very special cane indeed.

The cane didn't look like anything special. It was a standard Medicare-issue cane with an adjustable aluminum grip and a gray rubber tip, definitely unglamorous. Its purpose was to take some of the stress off Gran's mending hip, but Gran soon put it to another use as well—as an alarm bell of sorts when she wanted something or someone.

The household grew accustomed to hearing Gran's cane summoning them to whatever location she wanted them. Tap, tap, tap— always in threes—signaled that Gran needed someone to wait on her or assist her. If the response wasn't quick enough to suit her, the summons would be repeated, louder and more vigorously— thump, thump, thump, if necessary followed by *bang, bang, bang!*

Although the family lovingly and loyally helped Gran, knowing full well how much they owed her assistance, they resented the tapping cane somewhat. When Gran was finally summoned to heaven, the family retired her cane with admitted relief. It was stored in an upstairs closet just in case someone else might need it.

As it turned out, the whole family needed Gran's cane. Late one long winter night, a fire was caused by a malfunction in the electric dishwasher. Their batteries long since dead, the smoke alarms failed to warn the sleeping family. Disaster was narrowly averted when the family members were awakened by repeated trios of *bang, bang, bang* from Gran's old cane. The loud banging enabled the whole family to escape the flames just in time.

Had fiercely protective Gran's spirit returned to save her family? They think so. They still have that cane, too, which escaped the fire unharmed.

Spirits of Good and Evil

It all depends on whom you talk to and exactly what they saw or experienced. Is the white lady a healer or a witch? Or both at the same time? And what about the black dog that always accompanies the lady—is it the embodiment of evil, the guardian of a witch, or at least sometimes, a protector of the innocent?

This story has many venues. The lady and the dog are said to have shown up in many different locales in California. The tales from Fresno are typical. There are those who believe that the white lady and the black dog represent an old Spanish folk tradition, a myth about the nature of good and evil, about the human condition.

In this version of several incidents related by a family with deep roots in the San Joaquin Valley, the white woman and the black dog have been seen to appear under a huge, old pepper tree. The white woman is so called because she always is dressed entirely in white, though she has long, black hair and dark eyes. She seems to glow with an internal light. Her radiance is in sharp contrast to the enormous black dog that is always close by. Coarse, black fur covers its muscular body, and eerily glowing green eyes stare out at the rest of the world.

The woman and the dog have a habit of showing up during some sort of crisis or emergency. When, for example, a terrible car crash happened in the vicinity of the pepper tree, one of the victims later told how the woman appeared suddenly and was instrumental in helping the dazed victims escape the wreckage, just in time to lead them a safe distance away before the mangled cars exploded in flames.

"She saved our lives," one accident victim reported. "Who was she? I must thank her," he said as the ambulance departed the scene. But there was no one to thank. The woman and dog were gone.

On another occasion, a group of school kids was approaching a busy intersection. They weren't paying much attention to traffic as they excitedly pushed and shoved one another in some impromptu game. They were about to cross the road on a green light, when a truck swept around the corner without first stopping. Out of nowhere, the mysterious white woman stepped up and pulled a child from the truck's path, almost certainly saving a life. Once again, the woman and dog disappeared as quickly as they had arrived on the scene.

Once, when an old lady in the neighborhood lay dying in great pain from the cancer that was ravaging her frail body, the white lady materialized at her bedside. Silently, the figure offered a cup of tea to the old lady, who gratefully drank it. Afterward, she reported that she felt wonderfully better, her pain gone and her strength restored. It was a miraculous, if temporary, respite from her agony. The white woman was gone as abruptly as she had appeared, and this time the black dog was only briefly glimpsed in the background.

A pattern has been noted in these stories involving the white woman and the black dog. When the black dog is present but passive, under the control of its mistress, good things happen. If, however, the dog is evidently out of the woman's control and taking the lead, not-so-good things follow.

The aggressive stance of the dog, combined with a nerve-rattling snarl, sent one man stumbling out into traffic with fatal results one evening near the old pepper tree. On another occasion, the dog suddenly lunged away from the white woman's side and badly savaged a pregnant woman who couldn't run away fast enough.

One interpretation of the white woman and black dog stories is that this odd pairing symbolizes the dual character of imperfect humans. The white woman embodies the good side of our nature, while the black dog represents our darker impulses. While good and evil are real enough, the white woman and black dog exist only as spirits, or so the story goes. So watch out for the white woman and the black dog, and pray that the dog is under control.

Bibliography

Books

Ainsworth, Edward. *Beckoning Desert.* Englewood Cliffs, NJ: Prentice Hall, 1962.

American Automobile Association. *Southern California and Las Vegas.* Heathrow, FL: AAA Publishing, 2007.

Ault, Philip. *How to Live in California.* New York: Dodd, Mead, 1961.

Beckley, Timothy. *The UFO Silencers.* New Brunswick, NJ: Inner Light, 1990.

Botkin, B. A., ed. *A Treasury of American Folklore.* New York: Crown Publishers, 1944.

Clark, Jerome. *Unexplained!* Canton, MI: Visible Ink Press, 1999.

Coleman, Loren. *Mysterious America.* London: Faber and Faber, 1983.

Crow, John. *California as a Place to Live.* New York: Scribners, 1953.

Dorson, Richard. *American Folklore.* Chicago: University of Chicago Press, 1959.

Drury, Aubrey. *California: An Intimate Guide.* New York: Harper, 1947.

Federal Writers' Project. *California: A Guide to the Golden State.* Rev. ed. New York: Hastings House, 1967.

Guiley, Rosemary. *The Encyclopedia of Ghosts and Spirits.* New York: Facts on File, 1992.

Harper, Charles. *Haunted Houses: Tales of the Supernatural.* Philadelphia: J. B. Lippincott, 1930.

Hauck, Dennis. *Haunted Places: The National Directory.* New York: Penguin Putnam, 2002.

Jacobson, Dan. *No Further West: California Revisited.* New York: MacMillan, 1959.

Krantz, Les. *America by the Numbers: Facts and Figures from the Weighty to the Way-Out.* Boston: Houghton Mifflin, 1993.

Lewis, Oscar. *High Sierra Country.* San Francisco: Duell, Sloan, 1955.

Mack, John. *Abduction: Human Encounters with Aliens.* New York: Scribners, 1994.

Myers, Arthur. *The Ghostly Register.* New York: McGraw-Hill, Contemporary Books, 1986.

Pickering, David. *Casell Dictionary of Superstitions.* London: Casell, 1995.

Skinner, Charles. *American Myths and Legends.* Detroit: Gale Research Co., 1974.

Stein, George, ed. *The Encyclopedia of the Paranormal.* Buffalo, NY: Prometheus, 1996.

Taylor, Troy. *The Haunting of America: Ghosts and Legends from America's Past.* Alton, IL: Whitechapel Productions, 2001.

Thompson, C. J. S. *The Mystery and Lore of Apparitions.* London: Harold Shaylor, 1930.

Online Sources

www.Californiaghosts.com
www.worldreviewer.com

Acknowledgments

THIS IS MY SEVENTH BOOK COMPLETED UNDER THE EXPERT GUIDANCE and friendly counsel of Kyle Weaver, my editor at Stackpole Books. He was ably assisted by Brett Keener.

As she has done many times before, Heather Adel Wiggins has successfully captured the spirits of the stories in her haunting illustrations. For their valuable help, I thank the always friendly and helpful professional librarians at Rowan University's Campbell Library; the McGowan Library in Pitman, New Jersey; and the Gloucester County Library in Mullica Hill, New Jersey. The California Travel and Tourism Commission at Sacramento provided useful information and maps, as did numerous municipal chambers of commerce and visitors bureaus.

Again, as with nineteen previous books, my dear wife, Diane, provided both inspiration and support for this project. I could not have a more loving and understanding companion on our journey through life. Thanks again, my sweetheart.

About the Author

CHARLES A. STANSFIELD JR. TAUGHT GEOGRAPHY AT ROWAN UNIVERsity for forty-one years and published fifteen textbooks on cultural and regional geography. In the course of his research, he realized that stories of ghosts and other strange phenomena reflect the history, culture, economy, and even physical geography of a region. He is the author of *Haunted Vermont, Haunted Maine, Haunted Ohio,* and *Haunted Jersey Shore,* and coauthor with Patricia A. Martinelli of *Haunted New Jersey.*

Other Titles in the
Haunted Series

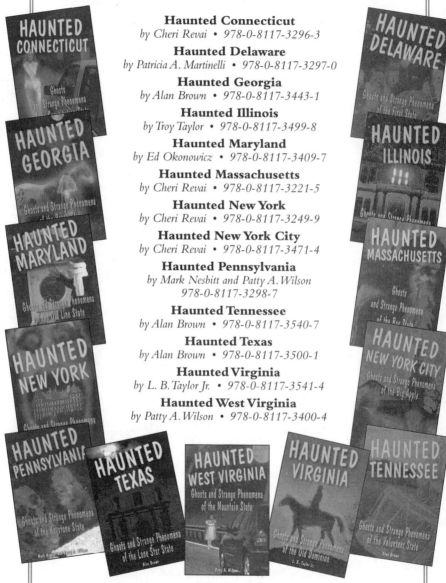

Haunted Connecticut
by Cheri Revai • 978-0-8117-3296-3

Haunted Delaware
by Patricia A. Martinelli • 978-0-8117-3297-0

Haunted Georgia
by Alan Brown • 978-0-8117-3443-1

Haunted Illinois
by Troy Taylor • 978-0-8117-3499-8

Haunted Maryland
by Ed Okonowicz • 978-0-8117-3409-7

Haunted Massachusetts
by Cheri Revai • 978-0-8117-3221-5

Haunted New York
by Cheri Revai • 978-0-8117-3249-9

Haunted New York City
by Cheri Revai • 978-0-8117-3471-4

Haunted Pennsylvania
by Mark Nesbitt and Patty A. Wilson
978-0-8117-3298-7

Haunted Tennessee
by Alan Brown • 978-0-8117-3540-7

Haunted Texas
by Alan Brown • 978-0-8117-3500-1

Haunted Virginia
by L. B. Taylor Jr. • 978-0-8117-3541-4

Haunted West Virginia
by Patty A. Wilson • 978-0-8117-3400-4